THE CHURCH IS PEOPLE

Bob W. Brown

BROADMAN PRESS
Nashville, Tennessee

4284-22 (BRP)
4255-63 (Paperback)

ISBN: 0-8054-5563-9

Dewey Decimal Classification: 262.7
Subject Heading: CHURCH

Library of Congress Catalog Card Number: 75-22506
Printed in the United States of America

Preface

Some folks keep talking about the institutional church. I'm never sure just what they mean. The church is not a denomination, or an organization, or a tradition, or a building. The church is people. Volunteer workers. Laughing people. Singing people. Hurting people. Sick people. Good and bad people. Strong and weak people. Attractive and repulsive people. An institution? Not the church that I have known and loved for more than forty years!

The people in this book are all fiction. They are all true. They are composite people put together by the author so no one will be embarrassed. No one knows any one of them, and everyone knows all of them.

Thanks to my family Helen, Jeff, and Amy who have shared my time. And to my staff of ministers who work with me: Rick, Enrique, Jim, Arthur. And to June Picklesimer who types it all, reads it all, and protects my schedule. Special thanks to our Trinity Church family who believes that the church is for everyone, believes it and practices it.

And thanks to our Lord Jesus who built his church big enough for everyone.

BOB W. BROWN

Lexington, Kentucky, 1976

To My Only Sister
June
And Joe and Kelly Joe
My Nearest Relatives and My Friends

CONTENTS

1
NORMA, SPIRIT-FILLED NORMA

"As you well know, Melvin and I were ready to get a divorce. At the time I thought it was all his fault. For years and years I had been suspicious that he was running around on me. I had gotten the anonymous phone calls, the whispers, and things like that. And there were times that he was out all night, or when he was supposed to be on the road, I couldn't find him in the motel where he was supposed to be.

"I became more and more suspicious. Suspicion is of the devil, one of the works of this world. Suspicion can come in on a person unless they have the whole armor of God on. I wear the armor now, Pastor, as described in Ephesians 6."

Norma was in my study for the umpteenth time trying to "convert" me to her new spiritual experience. She was a charismatic.

Norma was past forty and had been a member of our church for about ten years. She and her husband had been reasonably active. They brought their two children to Sunday School, and at various times Melvin had served on church committees. I knew about their marriage problems because I had counseled with them six or seven times. When they became involved in one of the extra-church groups in our city, I was surprised. When they became dedicated charismatics, I was really surprised. Somehow they just weren't the type. We should have learned that there is no "type" in anything religious.

"I begged Melvin to be a better husband. After all, we did have the two children. Even when I was being told by Satan that Melvin was running around with other women, I knew that Melvin loved the children. Finally I persuaded Melvin to go to a weekend spiritual marriage retreat. It wasn't difficult to persuade him, praise the Lord, because the Spirit was already at work.

"We went to this retreat. And I'll always praise the Lord for it. The first thing we did the first night was sit in rocking chairs in a candlelit room. Just Melvin and me. And Jesus. We were to rock for thirty minutes without talking. I was afraid that Melvin would go to sleep or get angry. But he just sat and rocked.

"Then we went into a spiritual group. Now you must understand that this is not like group therapy or some of those psychological things that worldly people do. This is not psychological at all. It is all spiritual. We have Spirit-filled leaders, and we have Spirit-filled people, and we invite the Spirit to come in himself. Praise the Lord!

"Don't think for one minute that this is just a bunch of emotional people either. At our first spiritual retreat we had a college professor, two doctors, two lawyers, and some well-known people in this town.

"Well that very first night one of those doctors was so filled with the Spirit that he began telling about his life. You would know him if I called his name. He told about the women he had slept with. Why he must have named by name a dozen or more. Oh, the Holy Spirit filled him. He just poured out his sin right there in front of twenty or thirty people. He didn't hold back anything. He was crying and his wife was crying. It was just beautiful! Praise the Lord.

"Then his wife broke into his testimony, and she began telling how she had hated him and was suspicious of him. And she told how she had also started having an affair with the insurance agent. She felt bad about that because the insurance man was young and he had a wife and little baby at home. The doctor's wife was so convicted that she poured it out. She even told who the insurance agent was. And God was at work because the wife of one of the lawyers there was the aunt of the insurance agent's wife. That just shows how the Spirit works. Praise the Lord.

"There was a pastor there. You would know him if I called his name. The Spirit came on him. He is not a Baptist incidentally, but he is pastor of one of the really big, I mean really big, churches in this town. He must have poured out his heart for an hour. He told about his doubts about his ministry. He didn't have any power or peace. His marriage was a wreck. His wife agreed to that. He was empty. Praise the Lord, I was there that night when the Spirit filled him. You probably know about it, Pastor, because he goes all over the country now telling the story. The same story that I saw happen. Every time he tells that story I just feel warm and gushy inside. He is so wonderful.

"Praise the Lord for Spirit-filled pastors.

"I've never been in a meeting like that. Finally, I just couldn't hold back any longer, and I told the group about Melvin and me. Oh, how I poured out my soul under the leadership of the Spirit. I've never felt so close to God and to his people. The more I talked, the more they helped me. They encouraged me to keep talking, to go ahead and cry, to just follow the Spirit. They hugged me and kissed me. We were all crying, laughing, praying, praising God.

"My life turned around that night. I was already saved, but I had never had the Spirit. But that night, praise the Lord, I got the Spirit. Oh yes, that night was the first time that I had ever seen anyone lift their hands when they prayed. How I love to lift my hands when I pray and sing. Oh, how I love to lift my hands. Why can't we teach our people to lift their hands in church when they pray and sing. Why?

"Back to the story. Melvin wasn't impressed. He did not confess his sins that night, and he did not pray for the Spirit. Just to show how the devil works, I became suspicious that night that Melvin was making a play for the doctor's wife—the one who had the affair with the insurance man. But praise the Lord, God used her the next afternoon to bring Melvin under conviction. At our Saturday afternoon meeting she was the very one who finally, by the Spirit, brought Melvin to confession and filling. I praise the Lord for her, and I've never been jealous of her or suspicious of her and Melvin for one minute. Not once. Praise the Lord.

"We knew after the retreat that there was so much more for us. We got into Bible study. The Spirit sent us a teacher. You have heard about him I know. He is more than a teacher, he is a prophet raised up by God for those last days. He is not a preacher. He has no seminary training. He doesn't need it, the Spirit bears witness with his spirit. I just can't describe to you what a fine teacher he is. Well, everyone needs Bible study, and this teacher had worked with some of the famous evangelists in this country. He has also taught in foreign countries. He made the Bible come alive.

"It was in this Bible class that we learned about prophecy and the end of time. Praise the Lord! We're living in the last days. He also introduced us to so many wonderful books about prophecy. Just think, when the Jews build a new temple in Jerusalem, Jesus will come. And I have read over and over that they will build the temple as soon as that silly problem with Egypt is solved. I just wish our country would give them money for the temple instead of money to fight the Arabs.

"I believe with all of my heart that I will be here when Jesus comes again. Of course I won't be here, right here; I'll be caught up in the rapture to meet the Lord in the clouds. I mean I will be on the earth when he comes. It will be in my lifetime. Praise the Lord!

"Just watch Jerusalem, Pastor. When that temple is done,

well, we will all be going up, up, and away." Norma smiled. She stopped talking for the first time and just sat there with a smile. She believes it alright.

I like Norma. I like Melvin. They are not trying to cause trouble in the church. They try hard not to become obnoxious to other people with their incessant conversation about their spiritual experience. But they are obsessed by it, and they have a sincerity that cannot be disputed or ignored. And their marriage has improved.

"I know that you do not believe in tongues. I've heard you say that the stories in Acts had to do with languages and that you think the only other New Testament reference to tongues is in Corinthians. And that you think it was one of the unpleasant problems in the Corinthian church. I know what you say about tongues.

"And some people continue tongue-speaking. I've seen them fake it out. And some of our people are too hung up on tongues. They try to get people to make funny sounds. Or they get people to close their eyes and just say 'Jesus, Jesus, Jesus' over and over again until they begin in tongues. I know these things have happened. I don't like that and real Spirit-filled people don't either. I mean people who are really filled with the Spirit. If tongues come, the Spirit gives them; you don't have to do anything; you just have to be willing and ready. I think you should know that Melvin and I neither one speak in tongues, but there are people in your church who do. Wonderful people. Praise the Lord!

"I also know what you think about healing. I know that when your dad was sick that some of our group came to you and offered to lay hands on your dad and anoint him with oil. He was dying in the hospital, isn't that right?"

I nodded in agreement. It was true. They came to offer the services of a spiritual healer. Dad was a chronic heart patient with a horribly damaged heart. He also had advanced cancer. He was seventy-three years old. Mother had died six months before. He was reasonably alert and not in too much pain. I was very devoted to my dad, and his dying was a painful experience.

They had come one evening late. I had been trying to keep my work caught up and stay with Dad. We were all tired and anxious. It was a tough time. They had come bouncing into my living room to see if I wanted one of their "healers" to go to the hospital the next day to heal Dad.

My reply had been: "How long will you heal him for? He is seventy-three. Will he be healed for two months, or five years, or twenty-five years? Will he be healed of heart disease and cancer and then die of something else in four weeks? What will you say to him? Maybe you will heal him so good that he will live to be 135 years old."

I invited the healers to go to the Shriners' Hospital and heal those crippled children. Some of these children were grotesque. Or perhaps the healer could come to the next meeting of the blind group in our church. We had more than fifty blind people in that group. Surely a blind person or a crippled child deserved as much attention as my dad. How did the healers decide when and who they would heal?

Norma said: "I heard all about that. At the time it made me mad. I thought you were rude to my friends. It showed a lack of faith on your part. But the more I thought about it, the more I understood what you were saying. Melvin and I eventually decided to back off on the healing thing, and now we are more willing to pray for the sick and let God take care of it in his own way. We never stopped believing in medicine. And we have wondered about the medical doctors who are charismatic. We don't understand how they can practice medicine and also believe in prayer and anointing at the same time. Of course, we have never asked them."

So I heard Norma out again. She is saying all of the things that the charismatics are saying. At this point Norma and Melvin are still my friends and still involved in the local church. They are having some serious internal struggles. Their experience has not produced the chaos and destruction that others have had.

There are churches that have been split and destroyed by the charismatic movement. There have been homes completely torn up and broken. Some of the charismatics have been so intense that their mates have left. One man told me that every time he even thinks about having sex with his wife that he just prays until the desire goes away. There have been sad stories of emotionally unstable people who have completely lost contact with reality under the influence of those spiritual meetings and have become emotional and religious basket cases.

If the charismatics have erred and become self-righteous in their judgements about the noncharismatics, it is just as easy for the "straight" Christians to err and become self-righteous about the charismatics.

Far too often and far too long our church life has been sterile and overorganized. We have been afraid of spontaneity and openness in worship and in church groups. We have taught our people to wear masks. We have ignored the freedom and joy that comes in our relationship with Jesus. We have allowed certain churches to become country clubs. We have tried to put people in boxes and label them. We try to make certain churches appropriate for certain people.

This kind of ecclesiastical manipulation paved the way for the charismatic movement in the main-line churches. We refused to recognize that people were different, their needs were different, and their gifts were different.

We are shocked to know that a six-figure-salaried businessman would pray "out loud" like a mountain preacher and that he really believes in "closed" communion. The most prominent lawyer in town enjoys country gospel, even in a morning worship service. The university dean will say "Amen" out loud when the preacher makes a good point.

And the doctor is fed up with church committees, budget campaigns, and twenty-nine church organizations.

Our comfortable and accepted status churches turned out to be wrong. We developed a status symbol ladder for denominations. Episcopal, Presbyterian, Lutheran, Disciples, Methodists, Baptists, Nazarenes, and the conservative groups for the very poor and unlearned. But that entire system changed and collapsed, and no one really noticed. It was in that collapse that the charismatic movement of the past decade took roots and prospered among these churches that were "up the social ladder."

Although many of the charismatics do have some profound and obvious personal problems, they are not all "sickies." Some of them are. Some of them are using this movement just like people have always used the church to see if it works. The excitement and the unusual about the charismatic movement will attract these troubled people. They also will be attracted by the promise of the spectacular and the sensational. Miracles are commonplace in the charismatic movement. The anxiety-ridden and guilt-possessed person wants a miracle. The charismatics deal in miracles.

There is an attraction because the charismatic movement is touched by mystery. They use a new language, new words, new feelings, new experiences. There isn't anything mysterious about teaching a fourth-grade class in a Sunday School. That's hard work. It's frustrating. Communion, a tired anthem by a poorly prepared choir, and a sermon on "Eight Reasons I Believe in God" are not mysterious. Much of our contemporary church life is in a rut. It is boring. It is hard work. The budget committee preparing next year's financial program is a poor comparison to a charismatic meeting with emotional testimonies about the miracles of that day.

One of the most important appeals of the charismatic movement is the open confession aspect of the movement. At some time nearly every charismatic will "tell his story." They confess real, and some imagined, sins. There is therapy in confession. It is a calamity when confession is made to a group of gossips. Some of the internal discussion within charismatic groups comes out of these confessions. For a variety of reasons, these confessions usually relate to sex. Some people like Norma and Melvin apparently were not hurt by the personal confessions. In other cases, it can be a disaster. Openness is a great idea, if you are open with people who can handle it, people who can be trusted.

The charismatic movement has also become respectable. The modern charismatic movement is a lot of doctors, students, and business people, rich housewives, Catholic priests, and Presbyterian teachers doing the same thing that the Holy Rollers have done for years and years. At one time these kinds of emotional and spiritual experiences were confined to the rural churches or the store-front churches in the cities. The main-line Christians had at one time or another, usually when they were teenagers, peeped in the windows of a Pentecostal church. Now they can see people doing the same thing at Notre Dame. And they can read about it from the pens of famous people. If money and education can gain respectability, the charismatics have it made.

Up until now the local church has been able to survive this new movement within the church. My hunch is that the enthusiasm of the charismatics will give the church some new impetus, that it will help us to desist from categorizing people and their religious experience. It will give the church a new vitality and flexibility.

Nothing will be accomplished by battle between the charismatics and the straight people. Each person, like Melvin and like Norma, must make their own pilgrimage. It is to be hoped that the church will be with them as they make that journey. We can walk together with the charismatics without becoming charismatic. The church is big enough. But the charismatic must resist his temptation to judge and criticize the noncharismatic, and the straight churchman must not judge the charismatic.

2

"POOR ME," SAITH IRMA

Irma was a neurotic. At least that is what some of the people in the church said. A generation ago people would have said that Irma was a "complainer" or that Irma always felt sorry for herself. Now that most popular magazines run articles about "nerves" people use a different language. Soap operas and even crime shows on television play up emotional and psychological deviations, and most Americans consider themselves well-informed about strange human behavior.

This is prevalent in the church, and one of the modern "ministries" is performed by the lay person who is always ready to discuss a "sick" person with another lay person. Pastors read a few books, and they begin to sprinkle psychological words in their sermons. Even if the people do not know just what the pastor means, and he may not know himself, it is a very pleasant and contemporary thing to do.

A man writes bad checks, and someone says that he is sick. A man robs the dry-cleaner shop, and someone says he is sick. A kid cheats on an algebra test, and he is sick. A fellow leaves his wife and two kids and marries a 1950 model blonde, and someone says he is sick. A deacon throws a fit in a deacons' meeting, and someone says he is sick. A student rebels about war, a woman agitates for the Women's Lib movement, or a church member joins the Jehovah Witnesses, and someone writes them all off as being sick.

In spite of the prevailing analysis among certain church women that Irma was sick, I still had to be her pastor. If she was sick, she wasn't sick enough to be put in a hospital. And it was certain that her husband Vincent wasn't going to take her to a psychiatrist. Vincent wasn't even going to do anything with Irma that Irma did not want done.

Maybe the story begins with Vincent. He was the classic henpecked husband. Everything about Vincent reeked with acquiescence. His countenance was poor. He rarely lifted his eyes to look at you and then the look was a glance. He was average size, but he slouched in a perpetual way that made him look small and drawn up. I always think of Irma being taller than Vincent, but she wasn't. He walked apologetically. Not a shuffle, just a hesitant walk. And he spoke the same way. A kind of "excuse me" tone of voice.

Someone told me that Vincent had distinguished himself in the Second World War. It was hard to imagine, and I was never able to keep a fix on that part of Vincent's life. I could not think of him in uniform nor could I imagine him as a war hero. My first and lasting impression of Vincent was a henpecked husband whose life was totally dominated by Irma.

Vincent had several brothers. Their mother had died when they were all at home, and the father had taught them to do the housework. The father had not married again, and each of the boys had taken his turn at the father's house until they married and left home. Vincent had been the last one to leave home. By that time he not only was an expert cook, but he was an excellent housekeeper.

Irma was an only child and her parents were older when she was born. At least they were older than most parents in their countyseat town. They were delighted when Irma was born, and they spoiled her with too much attention. When she was very young, she learned that she could keep their attention when she was sick. When she got into trouble with her parents, she could invariably escape their displeasure by feigning an illness or just by saying that her head hurt. By the time Irma started school, she had developed the pattern of complaining often to get attention or to escape punishment.

Her schoolteachers tried for twelve years to break that pattern. They were not successful. Irma missed tests because of sickness. She missed class plays, the prom, and ball games because of illness. Any school crisis sent Irma into a headache, stomach cramps, diarrhea, back pains, or shortness of breath. Her parents took her to various doctors and eventually they found a doctor who seemed to help. He would give Irma pills and sympathy. He always agreed that Irma "was not well."

After her parents died, Irma continued her job at the savings and loan. She had started to work there after graduation. Her uncle managed the savings and loan, and he was tolerant of her problems. When she had to miss work, her uncle didn't say anything. Everything was alright until her uncle died and a new young executive began making changes at the savings and loan. He was super-efficient. He made Irma nervous. She was uncomfortable with him, and her headaches increased in frequency and intensity. She had to miss work more often. The more work she missed, the more the young manager bugged her.

It was about this time that Irma went to the hospital for the first time. The doctors put her in for "tests" for ten days. While she was in the hospital, three important things happened. She decided to quit her job at the savings and loan. Vincent came to visit her; two days later he came back and brought her a box of Whitman's Samplers. The third thing, and the most important, was the diagnosis that Irma had a chronic nervous stomach. Irma knew that she wasn't well, and now she had an official diagnosis from a hospital to prove it. For the next twenty-five years Irma would tell people about her nervous stomach.

Irma lived on her modest inheritance from her parents.

She slept late, she watched television and read movie magazines. She went to church every time the door was open. Church was her recreation and her social life. Vincent attended the same church that Irma attended. They would talk to one another before and after the services. Eventually they began to sit together in church. The older people would tease them, and some of the older people thought they would make an ideal couple.

It was also about this time that Irma began gaining weight. She was eating a lot of sweets. She was eating between meals. None of this seemed to bother her nervous stomach. By the time Vincent proposed marriage, Irma had gained weight until she weighed more than two hundred pounds. She was too short to carry that much weight.

Irma miscarried during her first three pregnancies. She would eventually deliver two children and would always tell people that she had had five children and three of them had died. This always evoked sympathy from the listener. If the sympathizer asked Irma how old the three children were when they died, she would always say that they were "young, but you can still love them when they are young." Irma never said that she miscarried, she always said that her first three children had died. Vincent usually did not say anything in that kind of conversation.

Vincent got a job in a factory, and they lived a comfortable life with the two little girls. Vincent took care of the little girls, took care of the house, took care of Irma during her frequent illnesses, and did his work at the factory. He washed and ironed, cleaned the house and planted flowers. He did the grocery shopping, managed the money, and cooked breakfast every morning and prepared the evening meal. Irma usually fixed Sunday dinner after church. She occasionally invited church people home to eat with them.

Irma kept up with the aches and pains of the congregation. She used the telephone constantly. She called the members of her Sunday School class regularly and would dig out all of their troubles which she passed on to the pastor.

"Did you know that Mrs. Jackson's mother-in-law was down with arthritis again? Poor soul, she always suffers so much. I just don't know why Mrs. Jackson doesn't take her to another doctor. Of course, I understand about arthritis because I have serious arthritis in my left elbow. It developed soon after the third baby died. There isn't anything to be done in my case, but someone might be able to help Mrs. Jackson's mother-in-law.

"I was just talking on the phone to Lelia Asher. Her brother is a patient at the Baptist Hospital. Room 245. He is having tests run. He is a member of a Methodist Church here in town, but he doesn't go to church. The Methodists aren't much on visiting hospital patients. I told Lelia that you would go by and pray for him. It means so much to be prayed over while you are in the hospital. I guess I should know. I've been in the hospital fourteen times, and I know that I'm only here today because of prayer. That's room 245.

"I'm sure that someone has already told you, but Jane Doty is in the hospital and her father is sick at home. Jane is going to have surgery on her back. They wanted to do back surgery on me years ago, but no one, I mean no one, is going to do surgery on my back. I have suffered, no one knows how I have suffered, with my back. I just never tell Vincent or the girls about my back. Pastor, there are days that I can't get out of bed because of my back. But I would rather suffer than let them cut on my back. My Uncle Dave never could walk after they operated on his back.

"I realize that you are a busy, busy man. Our other pastor did not do all of the things that you do. Not that I'm complaining, you understand. The church wasn't as big as it is now. The smaller church was so nice. We all knew one another, and we helped one another. And when we called the other pastor he would always come. Now I know that the things you do in the city are important. And I know that other people need you more than I do. I've suffered so much alone, and I am used to it. But I have been down with my stomach for thirteen days. Just eating soup and Cokes. If you get a minute and are on this side of town, I wish you would stop by and just say a prayer. I do want to get back to church.

"The Lord never puts more on us than we can bear. But you know, Pastor, that I've surely had my share of troubles. I'm taking allergy tests now. The doctor says that I may be allergic to more than one hundred different things. He is very grave about it. I know that God will give me strength to bear it all. And they think that I have a very rare infection that affects the gall bladder. Just remember me in your prayer. If you're out this way, please stop by for a word of prayer.

"You know that I have suffered for more than twenty years and have been in the hospital more than fourteen times. I'm not one to complain. And I surely never call my pastor unless it is very important. Vincent and I have been faithful in supporting the church. I don't know of one time that we have ever given you a minute of trouble. You seem to get everything you want from the church. I've been in bed for nearly two weeks and my Sunday School teacher just called me. She didn't even know I was sick. She said that you did not even know I was sick. She said that you did not even mention my name in your prayer list last Sunday. I just don't understand how you could mention Jane Doty's father who isn't even a church member and not mention me. Not that I expected you to come by and pray, but the girls in my class didn't even know I was sick.

"Vincent is going into the hospital next Tuesday for a hernia repair. It is very minor surgery, and he will be home in a few days. My back is better, and we will get along very well. If you have time, stop by and see Vincent.

"I was so afraid this would happen. Vincent won't be home from the hospital for two more days, and my gall bladder is acting up. I just couldn't get to the doctor this morning so I took my medicine and went to bed. These attacks usually last four or five days. Could you get someone to bring Vincent home from the hospital. I don't expect you to get him, I know how busy you are. But one of the men in his class might get him. The girls can fix some soup and sandwiches, and we will get along alright.

"The nominating committee chairman asked me to help in the fifth-grade Sunday School department. I can't imagine what he is thinking about. I did teach children in Sunday School before I married Vincent. But I haven't been able, and you know that. I just can't imagine that young man asking me to teach in my condition. Of course, if the church wasn't so large, he would know my condition. But then Jane Doty is on the nominating committee and she knows my condition, not that she calls me or visits me like she use to. Now, I am perfectly willing to do church work, but I'm just not able. Vincent even had to resign as an usher because he has to be with me. Well, I just wanted you to know that the young man called."

Jane Doty wasn't the only church member who quit calling Irma. Eventually her circle of friends diminished until she became more lonely. The less attention Irma attracted, the more she tried to get attention with her illnesses.

Irma began creating scenes at church. The first time that she passed out at church, we were singing a hymn when she staggered down the aisle. People ran to her and kept her from falling. Everyone was afraid to move her. The rescue squad came and carried her out and took her to the hospital. Irma repeated this performance at least six times in the next eighteen months. Each time the rescue squad came, each time she was rushed to the hospital, each time she was sent home in a day or two.

Irma began talking about her heart condition. The doctors said that her heart was strong and well, but this kind of diagnosis did not deter Irma. She became convinced that she had actually had five heart attacks in church. She talked about her heart attacks sincerely. Although she was never in a coronary unit, she would tell people about her stay in the coronary unit.

Finally one of the doctors suggested to Vincent that Irma needed to quit taking so many pills that she was accumulating from so many different doctors. And he suggested that she go see a psychiatrist. Vincent was upset by the doctor's advice. Vincent did not feel comfortable suggesting anything to Irma. He was especially apprehensive about talking to Irma about her illnesses and her doctors. He felt, with reason, that Irma would explode if he told her she was taking too much medicine. She had become dependent upon her medicines. Probably no one knew for sure just what she was taking or how much.

Vincent did not want to tell Irma to go to see a psychiatrist. He said he did not believe she needed to see a psychiatrist, but even if she did, he didn't want to be the one to suggest it. He wanted me to talk to her about it, and I agreed to.

Irma agreed immediately. She told me that there was nothing at all to be ashamed of. She simply did not understand why some people acted so silly about psychiatrists. Many of the best known people in America went to psychiatrists regularly, and there was no stigma about it. She said that anyone knew that a person who has suffered like she had for more than twenty years and more than fourteen times to the hospital had reason enough to be under pressure and would probably need some psychiatric help. She would be glad to go as soon as Vincent could make the appointment.

"I don't know why in the world Vincent had you talk to me about it. He is just a silly goose, that Vincent is. This is the very thing. I have suffered so much, this will help me. Anyone who has gone through what I've gone through could be expected to need a psychiatrist."

A couple of weeks later at church I overheard Irma telling

some of the ladies: "My psychiatrist says that it is amazing that I've held up so well over the years with all that I have suffered. My psychiatrist says that it will take a while for me to get on top of my problem. A lot of people feel funny about going to a psychiatrist, but there is nothing in the world wrong with it. Some people go to a psychiatrist for years and years. With my luck I probably will have to go for years and years. Oh well, it's just another doctor, and God knows I have seen enough doctors in my lifetime. I doubt if anyone in our church has been to the doctors more than I have. But God will not put more on us than we can bear."

Every church has an Irma. Our nation is crowded with Irmas, and they often turn to the church for the kind of attention that they desperately need. Many of those people are stopped short of ending up in Irma's condition. Some place and sometime they get control, and they change their pattern. Others, like Irma, go down to the end of life always bidding for more attention. It is never easy for the family or church to know how to handle this kind of person. There are no pat answers. But it is a wasted life.

Fortunately more clergymen are being trained in pastoral care, and they are better equipped to handle the Irmas. Other churches are adding professionals to the church staff who have the training and skills to minister to Irma. Counseling is more visible and more important in the modern church than ever before. We may not be able to help Irma change, but we are at least trying to prevent this kind of wasted, miserable life.

3
LEE'S PERSONAL PROBLEM

"It was all so simple to Papa. He wasn't reared in a church-going family. Not that his people were wicked or against the church. They just didn't attend church. Maybe they didn't believe. When I was young, I thought that everyone believed in God. And when I said it, I believed it myself. It was all so natural to me. I can't remember any time in my life when I didn't believe. Now that all of this has happened, I'm not sure at all that everyone believes, maybe no one believes. In either case, it has never been simple. But Papa made it all seem so simple."

Lee was in my office. He had been there for two hours. It was a strange interview. Lee and I had been friends, good friends for more than twenty years. We had attended college and seminary together. We had been reared in the same part of the country. We had exchanged pulpits, sat up all night in long, intimate conversations. We got together at conventions and meetings. Everyone would say that we were "best" friends. And we were. We are.

I watched his familiar face and saw the perplexity and the pain. I could read Lee. I know him so well. I can anticipate his lines, what turns him on. Over the years we have deliberately built our friendship becaure we need each other. It has not been casual, it has been a genuine friendship built on mutual need and mutual trust. There is no one I trust more than Lee. We have never had secrets. If everyone needs a trusted friend, and they do, Lee and I have been fortunate.

He has a lot going for him. He always had some things going for him that I didn't have. He was and is a good-looking fellow. In college he was an outstanding athlete and campus leader. His grades came easy. He was the "Who's Who" type guy. Somehow he was always able to get more done than any three fellows in our dorm. He could play on the teams, get elected to the offices, date the girls, and make top grades in his classes. He had a church during college, and the church prospered. Everything he did turned out right. One of the freshmen said that "Lee reeked with success."

Lee worked hard and that multiplied his natural talents. He wasn't lazy. He always did more than anyone expected. He never rested on his laurels; he never rested. The past eight or ten years it hit me that Lee never rested. He was always doing something, always on the move, always into something. I wondered privately what was driving Lee. When we passed forty, I was already thinking about retirement, about grandchildren, about sitting on the porch. But then I was always slower and more introspective than Lee. It could correctly be said that I never was too ambitious and that made me reluctant to criticize Lee for his obsessive drive.

Lee has the big church. The really big church! His salary is one of the top salaries; his staff is large and adequate. His church is one of the key churches in our denomination. He gets all kinds of speaking engagements and denominational assignments. In his city he is "Mr. Religion." They all know him and respect him. Lee isn't flamboyant or phony. He has a lot of integrity. He is a man of enormous talents, and he uses every gift in every way. Recognition has come to him with all that means to an ambitious pastor.

If you are successful in the ministry, there are numerous fringe benefits. The popularity and recognition feeds your ego. The fellows like Lee have a good-sized ego to begin with. I know him well and I know that his ego is big, but no one has ever accused him of being pompous or conceited. He handles it well. With all of his self-confidence, he can be humble and condescending without being patronizing. He's an unusual man.

Lee lives good. In addition to his big salary, he travels a lot. He has been places that I've never been. Not that travel is that important to me, but it is to him. Some of the rich people in his church have given him some fantastic gifts. A cabin. Good stock certificates. Valuable articles for his house. Big cars. Flying lessons. A boat. Investments. He can move with the country club set in his city, and you might find him at midnight in a slum house praying with a dying, poor old man. He can visit in the drunk tank at the jail and eat lunch with the mayor.

A long time ago I quit trying to figure out what made Lee tick. Like most other people who knew him, I just accepted the fact that he could get more done than anyone else that I have ever known. He amazes me, and I love him as a friend for more than twenty years. I don't really envy him, although by every standard of pastoral achievement, he has long since surpassed my meagre accomplishments. Some of our contemporaries are jealous of Lee and critical of him for obvious reasons. He ignores these critics, and he continues our friendship, although I'm a denominational "nobody." And these two facts also say something important about Lee.

I was an usher at Lee's wedding. It was another proper thing in Lee's life. I have always thought that Roslyn was the best thing that ever happened to Lee. They seemed to complement each other. Ros was a campus leader, too. She was the kind of girl that used to be described as a "handsome woman." She wasn't frilly or fixy. She wasn't striking. No one in school ever called Ros beautiful, or sexy, or glamorous. She wasn't hard or tough, but she wasn't gushy or aggressive. Ros didn't come on strong. She wasn't loud, she wasn't withdrawn. You always knew when Ros was around, but her presence didn't really change things. When Lee joined a group, everything changed and pointed toward Lee. I've always liked Ros, but always felt that she kept me, and everyone else, at a safe distance. That's OK, too.

Lee and I never talked much about Ros. But I've never talked to him much about my wife. I'm not much on talking about my wife to anyone. I talk to my wife about everyone. I'll tell her all about this conversation with Lee. She likes Lee, she approves of our friendship, and she has always been jealous of the things that Lee and Ros have that we will never have. My wife, like most women, has always been charmed by Lee.

Ros presented Lee with three children. Now, Lee does talk about his children. This is his tender spot. It has always been his most obvious emotion. When Lee talks about his kids, he turns on. He is intense, animated, and excited when he talks about his children. I've always figured that I loved my own kids but somehow I've never been as excited about my children as Lee is. This has been a private confusion to me. My kids have been loved, and they act like they know it. They always act like they love me. But I'm not capable of Lee's excitement and sentiment about my kids. I guess that has perplexed me more than anything else about my complex friend.

Well, that's Lee. And that's something about Lee and me. You can understand now something about my feelings when Lee began his monologue about his papa. I felt comfortable. We are old friends. We have understanding. At least that's what I thought.

"Papa joined the church a few weeks before he and Mama were married. It was just the natural and right thing for Papa to do. How many times I've heard Papa say that we all knew the right thing to do. Papa always divided life up that way. Do the right thing. He never talked much about the wrong thing. He didn't talk about it, because he didn't have a place or time for the wrong thing. When I went to Papa for advice, it was always right. When Papa spent money, voted in an election, attended a church business meeting, decided to buy a car—whatever he did, Papa was always so right.

"His entire church life was that way. Papa did not struggle with church decisions or religious questions. He ran the store. He paid his debts. He gave credit to some people, refused credit to others. He made some money, made some friends, and made some enemies. He integrated his religion into running the store, and somehow everyone expected it. He always went to church and always went to the store. He always came home for lunch and always took a nap.

"Papa opened the store at 8:00 A.M., and he went to Sunday School at 9:30 A.M. He closed the store at 6:00 P.M., and we ate supper at 6:15 P.M. We went to Sunday and Wednesday night church at 7:30 P.M. If Papa ever questioned the virgin birth, or healing, or the purpose of prayer, he never mentioned it. He didn't read the Bible much, but he believed it. He believed all of it. No questions. No doubts.

"When Mama died, Papa was unbelievable. They had been married forty-two years. It was a great marriage. One of the all-time great marriages. I thought I would just die when Mama died. And I dreaded seeing Papa. All the way in on the plane, I kept dreading seeing Papa. I felt that fear and dread more than I felt Mama's loss. Papa was just great. He said that Mama had gone to heaven. She had died suddenly and peacefully. She hadn't suffered a minute. She died in her sleep. Papa accepted it so beautifully. So quietly. With so much faith and trust. It was so simple to Papa.

"He went right on after Mama's funeral. My brothers and I tried to arrange things for Papa, but he did not let us. He didn't need our interference. He just lived like he had always lived. Except without Mama. After forty-two years! He expected to go be with her soon. It was just the kind of thing that we preach about. All of the stuff we say about faith, about love, about heaven. Papa really and truly believed it. He believed all of it.

"Cancer killed Papa. After they diagnosed it, he called me to come home. He told me and the other boys that he did not want them to do a lot of painful and expensive things to prolong his life. He said he had had a long, good life. He was lonely without Mama. He was proud of his sons. He had all that any man could ever want or expect. God had been good to him. He had made friends, earned enough money in the store to raise his family. He said that he and Mama had been so happy. He had served his church the best that he could, had seen seven grandchildren born. Papa smiled and said he had caught some big fish and some had gotten away. He was ready to go and be with Mama and Jesus. He didn't want them sticking him full of holes.

"Papa died in a week. I was there. He really was ready to go. He didn't exactly give up, he just resigned himself to death. And he died."

I knew Lee's mama and papa. They were just like Lee had described them. There was a lovely simplicity about the family, and Lee's drive had come from someplace else.

Lee paused. Tears glistened in his eyes and one or two big tears ran down his cheek.

"Now it gets tough. Papa would never in a million years understand. I'm not sure you will, but someone has to listen. For three years now I've been getting into a bind. A terrible, terrible bind."

Lee's face was contorted now with a different kind of pain. I began to feel sick. I had never before seen Lee show that kind of feeling. It was anguish.

"It's a woman, my friend. Me, Lee, the guy with all of the answers. Now I'm hung up on a woman and I'm ready to give up the church, give up Ros and the kids, give up my life such as it is, and marry the woman. Not only am I ready to do it, I want to do it. I've never wanted anything as bad in my life. Never. Never.

"Her name is Betsy. I've known her about a year. She isn't a member of my church. We met through one of those committees in the city that I got myself put on. I know this sounds like sixteen-year-old stuff, but the first day we met, something happened. I changed my schedule that very first day. She completely fascinated me. I talked to her for hours. I dreamed about her, contrived ways to see her again, and of course, those schemes worked. We have met in every legitimate and clandestine way and place imaginable. It's gone on for months, and I'm about to crack.

"I'm not stupid. Every pastor has gotten in a mess about women. There are always designing women in a church. There are always people who will gossip and slander a preacher about women. And God knows that there are always pastors who get trapped. Some of them get involved with a woman without premeditation, and some of them just plan to chase women. That's their style. And I've always had some sympathy for preachers who get smeared with a woman story. I have tried to help some guys out who were guilty, but I don't want to be the one to throw the first stone.

"Anyway, I always figured I could handle it. I thought I was smarter than the others, and I had my own devices to handle sticky situations. And I always had Ros and the kids. And I could always remember Papa and his talk about doing what is right. More than that I believed in God. I wasn't about to go against God. So when things would get tight or sticky with some gal in the church, I could handle it. Man, I've never been in a jam over a woman. Not once!

"Now I'm in love with another woman. Another man's wife, in fact. She has two children herself. I want to be with her. I want to tell her everything I do, I want to try my ideas out on her. I want to make her laugh, or have her cry when I cry. I respect her judgement. I think she is beautiful, I want to touch her. Live with her. I'm in torment. When I talk to her, I feel great.

"But there is no way. I can't do it to Ros and the kids. I can't do it to Betsy's husband and her kids. I can't do it to Mama and Papa and to a few thousand people who for twenty years have respected me and listened to me. There are just too many people. Good people. If I hurt them and disappoint them, I will become bitter. You know what? More than Ros, more than the kids, more than Mama and Papa, more than the church members, I just can't give up the ministry. I'm more sure of my call to the ministry than I'm sure of anything. I've had offers to do other things. I've been so discouraged and so angry with my job that I've thought of quitting a thousand times. But I am absolutely sure that the only really right thing for me is to be pastor of a church."

Lee smiled, "Papa would understand that line about the right thing.

"I can't quit. I can't give up my family, and I have so far been incapable of giving up Betsy. I can't give up the ministry. And I can't have it both ways. But it's tough, my friend, it's tough."

Lee is in pain. I'm not sure what all is operating here. I know how I would counsel a church member who came with the same story, and I've heard enough of these stories. But this isn't one of my members. This is my best friend. I love him and respect him. I feel for him. I haven't been where he is, but I know he is telling me the truth. I know that his feelings are honest. If the church gets a hint of the story, they will fire him. If Ros finds out, she will divorce him. If the story hits the city, the skeptics will laugh him out of town. Lee's position is so fragile. Every pastor has such a delicate and small margin for error, for humanness. There is no job in the world like the pastor's job. No one is so restricted and no one is so confined. Any other professional can endure and outlast gossip, suspicion, divorce, or adultery. But not the pastor. Not Lee.

But he knows that. They all know it, if they don't know

it, they learn it in their first church. They learn it the first time the gossip mongers start. They learn it the first time someone sets them up for "a story." Some of them are driven out of the ministry by the gossip. Some of them simply cannot endure the suspicion. Some of them have a bad marriage, and they get their divorce and another job. Some of them do get involved with their own Betsy, and it kind of wears itself out and no one ever knows or ever talks. Some like Lee, make a deliberate conscious decision, and they reject Betsy and they stay in the ministry. With a troubled conscience probably.

With all of his success and status things, Lee evidently found things in Betsy that he needed. Things Ros would not or could not give him. And there will be a thousand times that Lee will wonder. And wonder.

My friend left my office. He will be back in his pulpit. Back in the hospitals, the funeral homes, and in his study. He will continue meeting with committees at church, counseling people in broken marriages, preaching in revivals, marrying couples, and working too many hours. He will probably work harder, pray more, and preach better. He will plan budgets, and buildings, read the Bible, and work with his people. The church members will never know how near they came to a crisis. They will never know and never really understand that their pastor was in the throes of an all too human conflict.

There will be times when he thinks about Betsy. When he weeps. Times when he is frustrated with the church, with the people, with Ros, and the kids. Times when he feels trapped. Times when he is afraid to even think. Nothing is ever simple. Even Lee's papa could have told him that. Nothing is simple, and those who give their life to the church are not taking a path of simplicity. They are taking a road that is by description "narrow." It is a road cluttered with our humanity and weakness, by our broken pieces, by our failure.

Lee is not a hero or villain. He is just another of the countless millions who at one time or another have faced some hard, emotional, profound decisions about the church. He is another one of us who must walk in the church with feet of clay. Another one of us who get into complex and difficult situations but find that the church is indeed the light in the tunnel. Lee is another one of us who is intrigued by and held by the church. He can't let go of the church.

Had Lee left the church, the church would survive and go on. And the true church would never leave Lee.

4
EULA MAY'S CHURCH

They always called it "Eula May's Church." Eula May always called it "My Church." When the met sat around in Tike Dillon's Saloon and talked about the town, they often came around to discussing "Eula May's Church." When the Methodist women had a meeting to pray for missionaries and plan the ice cream social, they often talked about "Eula May's Church." Of course the Methodists, and the men in Tike's Saloon, knew that it was a Baptist church. But Eula May had supplanted the Baptist name in the community.

It was a small church in a small town. When I arrived to preach my "trial" sermon, Eula May and Hubert, her husband, were already at the church. Tom Wire was building up the fire in the old furnace. While the auditorium and Sunday School rooms were warming up, Tom was sweeping off the pulpit. Eula May was sitting on the front row advising Tom about the furnace and how he should get there earlier. Seemed that she and Hubert had waited more than twenty minutes for Tom's arrival.

I had not met anyone from the church prior to that Sunday. One of my teachers had sent me there for the "trial" sermon. He said that this church usually had student pastors, and they were looking for a new pastor. The student pastors normally stayed about two years. The teacher had preached there on various occasions and the people usually took his recommendations.

He told me: "It's just a small church in a small town.

It is a good place to get experience. The church won't change much or grow much, no matter what you do. The best family in the church is Eula May and Hubert Morris. They will take you under their wing. They don't have any children and they have always found their fulfillment in showing kindness to student pastors."

I walked on to the front of the church and introduced myself to Eula May Morris. She was a middle-aged woman, perhaps forty-five to fifty. She could have been thirty-five or fifty-five, but I calculated her about fifty. She was dressed well in conservative and expensive clothes. Eula May was composed and looked me over with a practiced eye. I felt like I was being examined by a physician or a salesman, or perhaps a detective. I felt uncomfortable.

Eula May told me to sit down. I sat. She did not introduce me to Hubert or Tom. They both were looking at me and I felt that I should speak to them, but when Eula May said, "Sit," I automatically sat.

The conversation was to the point. It was like Eula May was delivering a monologue that she had rehearsed, or maybe she had given the same speech before. It went like this!

"Our church, the Pleasant View Baptist Church, is one of the oldest Baptist Churches in the county. It was organized in the early part of the last century, 1798 to be exact, by a courageous group of Baptists who came down the river from Fort Boonesboro. One of the first things they did after building a stockade to defend themselves from the savages, was to build a Baptist church. My great grandfather William Wade was one of the founders of our church. From 1798 until now there has been a Wade in our church. My brother, who died four years ago, was a member here. His son Albert William is a member here, although he teaches school in Lexington and is not able to attend often. He mails me his tithe each month. I am the only Wade who lives here now.

"Our town, Pleasant Valley, has changed. At one time this was one of the most lovely farming areas in the state.

People were prosperous, and they attended church. The church has always been called Pleasant View because it overlooked this beautiful valley. But that has all changed.

"Before I was born the railroad came through here, and they eventually placed that ugly rail yard at the north end of the valley. I'm sure you heard the railroad noises, saw the filth, and smelled the stinking smells from the yards. In addition to bringing that dirt and noise, the valley filled up with immigrants who worked from the yards. Some of them are Italians, some are colored people, but most of them are Germans. As you know most Germans are Catholic."

Eula May had not stopped for breath. She had not asked any questions. She did watch me while she was lecturing, but her eyes did not seek a response. I was being told.

"Our church has been a faithful witness to Jesus Christ in this valley for nearly more than 150 years. We have never compromised our beliefs for one minute. We are not a large church, but as I always tell our young pastors, there are no small churches. Our church has been the most important building in this valley for more than 150 years. With the infiltration of trash the past few years, the church has been more important than ever.

"I am on the pulpit committee. Leon Taylor and Raymond Turley are the other two members of the Committee. Leon, Raymond, and my husband Hubert are the Deacons. My brother was a deacon when he died four years ago. We have not replaced him for the simple reason that we do not have a man who is scripturally qualified. One of the strengths of our church has been in our deacons. We have never elected a man as deacon who was not scripturally qualified. Incidentally, the deacons normally meet at my house on the first Sunday of each month. You can plan to meet with them. They will meet today.

"I have been church clerk since I was sixteen years old." She smiled for the first time and said: "It was said that I was the youngest church clerk in Kentucky. I keep an accurate membership roll with all of the addresses and phone numbers. I also keep careful records of the business meetings. Because of my experience I also help the moderator, my brother was moderator until he died four years ago, conduct the business meetings in correct parliamentary order. Incidentally, one of the most important parts of running a church is to keep parliamentary procedure in all business meetings. In our church we use Roberts Rules of Order, and we stick to Roberts. I always bring a copy of Roberts to the business meetings. If the pulpit committee decides to recommend you, we will have a business meeting to vote on you tonight.

"We have found that it is best for the pastor to come by my house when he arrives on the church field each week. I keep up with what is going on in the valley and I can tell him who needs a visit from the pastor and just what he needs to do. Of course most of our pastors eat their meals with me. I have a room in the house that the pastor can sleep in. It is just like the Old Testament story of the godly woman who kept a prophet's room. You might like to know that the pastor of Pleasant View has stayed with the Wades for more than seventy years, with but few exceptions.

"Well Hubert, you and Tom should be about done getting the church ready. Tom, it is time to ring the bell. I'm going back to get my classroom ready. A good Sunday School teacher is always the first one in her room." Eula May got up and left me sitting on the front row. Tom and Hubert ignored me. Tom rang the bell, and Hubert disappeared out the front door of the church. I sat on the front row as some people began to drift in.

Eula May came back through the door leading to the Sunday School rooms. "I neglected to tell you that Hubert, my husband, is the church treasurer. He will give you a check tonight after the evening service. You will eat lunch with us, and we will talk some more about the church."

It did not seem appropriate at that time to tell Eula

May Morris that I had other plans for lunch. And I didn't think it was important. I had other things on my mind. Here I was about to be considered and voted on for my first church, and my introduction had been her monologue. She was a member of the pulpit committee, but she had asked nothing of me. She had not asked anything about my personal life, she had asked nothing about my plans or programs for the church, or what I believed. I decided that she already had that kind of information from the teacher and when I met with the pulpit committee that afternoon there would be time for serious discussion.

The morning worship was interesting, but that is another story. Several people came by to speak to me. Eula May waited until most of the worshipers had left then she announced: "I am going home now to get our lunch ready. Hubert will ride with you and direct you to my house." Casually, but courteously, I told Eula May that I had made other plans for lunch, but I would be back in time for the pulpit committee meeting.

Her expression changed immediately. She never had a pleasant look on her face, at best she was tolerant. But now her countenance changed. She was angry. I would learn to recognize that anger and would eventually learn to anticipate it. That first morning however it surprised me. She proceeded to lecture me severely. She said that she had prepared dinner for three, and I was the third one. It was rude and thoughtless to decline her invitation. The pastor always ate Sunday dinner with her. She had already told me that and she was sure that my teacher had also told me. But if I preferred to do something else at dinnertime that was entirely up to me. "Come on Hubert, we will go home." With that she stomped out of the church building with Hubert trailing. No mention of the pulpit committee meeting.

I knew that I had made a mistake with Eula May, but I had planned to meet my girl friend and her parents for lunch in an adjacent city. When I went to my automobile, Raymond Turley came over to tell me that the pulpit committee would meet with me at Eula May's house at 2:30. "She don't mean 2:35 either. Eula May is a mighty good cook, you're going to miss a good dinner. Ain't nobody in the valley can fix a roast like Eula May."

At 2:25 I drove up to Eula May's house. Leon Taylor and Raymond Turley were sitting in the yard talking to Hubert. I joined them. We made small talk about baseball, weather, the economy, and politics for about forty-five minutes. The three men were obviously ill at ease. Eula May did not appear. Hubert excused himself and went in the house.

"Eula May has taken to bed with one of them sick headaches. Said she don't feel like talking to the preacher. She said it was up to you all if you want to recommend him. She thinks he preached right well, but he is awful young and inexperienced." Hubert looked embarrassed. "She says that it is alright with her if the church wants to call him."

Leon and Raymond were confused. They didn't really know what to do and had no inclination at all to say anything to my face that would be personal. They talked some about the Sunday School and said that they usually paid the preacher 60 percent of the Sunday offering, although at times they had paid a salary. Leon said that the church didn't take in much money, but they always figured the young preachers were glad to get the experience.

That night the church called me as pastor without a dissenting vote. Eula May was not there, but Hubert voted for me. I had the feeling that Eula May's absence created more interest than voting on a new preacher.

My trouble with Eula May had begun. The following Sunday she confronted me in front of a dozen people. Her voice was shrill when she said: "I fixed lunch for you yesterday. You did not show up. I warmed it up for supper. You did not show up. It was past eight o'clock at night when

I found out that you had been out with Raymond Turley! His wife said that you were visiting church members. How in the world could you be visiting church members when I am the clerk and I have the church roll. I wanted to tell you that Mrs. Savage was sick and needed a pastoral call."

She had made me mad, but I tried to answer her calmly. "Mr. Turley knows where some of the members live. He volunteered to go visiting with me and introduce me to some of the people. We went to the hospital to see Mrs. Savage."

"Raymond Turley has no business running around on Saturday doing the work that you are paid to do. And paid well, incidentally. Raymond Turley has a wife and four children to take care of, and he needs all of the time he can get to take care of his family. If you can't do your work without taking a man away from his family, maybe we need to find someone who can."

Eula May stood with her hands on her hips glaring at me. She was mad. I was mad, too.

"Will you, or will you not be at my house for dinner today?" Eula May challenged me.

I knew by now that eating at Eula May's house was a big thing to her, and my hunch was that it was also a big thing in the valley. All day Saturday in my visits to the church members people had been subtly complaining about the way the church "was run." Only one person had called it "Eula May's church," but the implications were clear. Apparently the best hope for the church was to break her influence. Stand up to her. I was young and cocky. I didn't like her, and I didn't want anyone controlling my life so it wasn't hard to defy her.

"No, I will not be eating lunch with you today. Or next weekend either," I told her.

By worship time, the gossip had gone all through the Sunday School that the new preacher and Eula May had

had a fight. The preacher wasn't going home with her. Just before church began Raymond Turley gave me a big wink and the teenagers moved off the back row and sat in the choir. We had more in the choir than we had in the pews. Eula May sat in her customary seat and listened to my sermon with a twisted, silly smirk on her face.

A few weeks later I announced from the pulpit that we would begin work on a Christmas program.

After church she came for me. Mad again. Madder than I had ever seen her. Madder than I had ever seen anyone at any time.

"We do not have Christmas programs in this church. We do not celebrate Christmas. It is pagan. If you knew your Bible at all you would know that our Lord was not born on December 25. That date is a pagan date. Our Lord was probably born in April, but you do not know that much about God's Word! All you care about is pleasing the crowd. Appealing to children with your stupid stories and your plans for basketball teams, hay rides, and weiner roasts! I told you that this church stuck to the Bible!"

She was shouting and seething. "I have seen Christmas plays in churches. A china doll in a manger. Nothing but an idol, a graven image. Fools dressed up in bed sheets pretending to be angels. More fools in bathrobes acting like shepherds. And even more fools with jewelry around their necks acting like the three Wise Men.

"I will not have it at my church! As liberal as you are, you are probably planning to bring a Christmas tree in the church building. Or perhaps Santa Claus. Santa Claus is a lie, a way of deceiving children, a way of replacing Jesus. If people loved Jesus like they love Santa Claus, our world would be a different place. You will not get away with this!"

Eula May stopped. She was up in my face. She was daring me to answer.

"We're going to have a Christmas program, Mrs. Morris.

We're going to act out the Bethlehem story with shepherds, Wise Men, and angels. And we're going to have a tree, and we're . . ." but I didn't get to finish.

Eula May Morris slapped my face. She hit me hard. My ears rang. Before I could duck or react in another way, she hit me again on the nose. With some composure, she turned and walked away.

"Let's go home, Hubert," she called. Her voice sounded calm, but commanding.

The next business meeting we voted to have a Christmas program. Eula May and Hubert abstained, and she wrote in the minutes that the vote was not unanimous, that there were several abstentions.

Eula May never hit me again. She disagreed with me publicly at business meetings. She criticized me continuously to the people. She opposed the special programs for young people, she criticized the Vacation Bible School, she objected to the Catholic children participating in the programs for the youth. She said that I didn't preach the Bible. She objected to the reorganization of the Sunday School, she was openly hostile to the election of four new deacons. The deacons quit meeting in her house. She spoke at length against raising my salary, against painting the church building, and against adopting an annual budget.

Eventually her influence in the church diminished and the church grew away from her power permanently. When I left, she attended services rarely and had become a lonely, bitter, old woman. The church had been her life. She did not respect Hubert. She did not have friends. The church was her domain. At one time her family had presided over the valley, but their kingdom had changed when the railroad yards were built. They had adapted to that change and had taken control of the church. Eula May had felt that her control in the church was her destiny. It was her divine right. It never occurred to her that other people loved the church as much as she did and that they had some rights, too. She just never thought about it. It was her church, and she knew what was best.

Many church bosses are like Eula May. For a variety of reasons they assume a divine right of rule in a church. It may be that they assume that other church members have less interest and less concern about the church. The unconcern of many members enhances the self-esteem of the ones who want to rule. They take over a church because other members default.

Eula May was not happily married. Often the church boss is frustrated in a miserable marriage. She had tried Hubert, and he was found wanting. Hubert and Eula May rarely talked about anything. They had slept in separate bedrooms for years. He never asserted any independence, because he was afraid of her rages. Hubert did not realize that the rages were indicative of her frustration with his weakness. If Hubert had been a stronger person, Eula May would not have felt compelled to challenge the pastor and the church members.

Often the church boss is not only frustrated in a marriage, but frustrated in his work. Every church has had some member who tries to take control, because the church is the only place that he has any control or influence. In his work he is constantly being told what to do by someone else. This is especially true of middle income industrial and commercial workers. They get locked into a certain kind of job in an hierarchy of bosses. There is always someone looking over their shoulder. Evaluating. Judging. Appraising. Giving orders. But it's not that way at the church. At church there is no hierarchy. Everyone is free before God to express his opinion. And in the spirit of compromise and the frantic desire of pastors to keep peace at any price, the squeaking wheel gets the grease.

After Eula May had about dropped out of church, Raymond Turley told me a story. He said that he had always "kind of felt sorry for Eula May." Seems that when she was young, one of Turley's uncles had carried on a torrid love affair with her. Raymond described the uncle as a ladies' man who traveled widely. The uncle was handsome and glib. He was too sophisticated for Eula May, and he had promised marriage for sex. She had reluctantly, then enthusiastically responded. The uncle had told the younger Raymond the details of the love affair. Without announcement or warning, the uncle left the valley. Shortly thereafter, Eula May married Hubert.

Raymond told me that the uncle had turned up in the valley every year or two. Every time the uncle came back he would call Eula May. Raymond said that they would meet some place. He thought that they had stayed together in a hotel for several days at a time over the years.

I was surprised at Raymond's attitude. He was very calm and sympathetic. "Every time Eula May got mean with someone, I figured she was just taking out her broken heart on them." Eula May was also carrying a heavy load of guilt.

We soon learn in the church that some of the most irritating and abrasive members are carrying guilt. They handle their guilt by picking fights in areas where they feel confident and guiltless. Eula May could be outspoken and rigid about Christmas, ball teams, or youth activities. She could be strict about parliamentary procedure and the church record book. But Eula May was vulnerable about adultery and doubtless would have gone into orbit over sex education in the church.

It is difficult for the church to go around Eula May and her kind. At times, an encounter and a showdown seem inevitable. In other instances, the congregation and the pastor can avoid these ugly confrontations. Some church bosses weary of the battle and drop out of that role; they often drop out of the church. And others dominate or run off the pastor and the other leaders in the church.

Church conflict is as old as James and John, as old as Barnabas and Paul, as old as the Jerusalem Conference in

Acts 15 and Galatians 2. It is always painful. As long as the church is people, there will be people like Eula May who want to run the church. There will be people like Raymond Turley, who for a variety of reasons allow the bosses to boss. There will be confrontations when someone will win and someone will lose. All of this we can expect. We cannot expect perfect peace or harmony. And we will never find an adequate answer to the question, Who runs the church?

5
IT PAYS TO SERVE JESUS

I grew up with the Bobby Brady stories. Bobby was my dad's first cousin, and he was a kind of hero to my dad. At the time that Dad needed a hero (my grandfather had died when Dad was seven) Bobby just filled the role. He was clean, friendly, witty and a great baseball player. When I was born, they named me after Bobby.

Bobby became ill and died soon after I was born. He was just a young man in his thirties. He was survived by his wife and daughter and many admirers. Dad told me numerous times that Bobby had the largest funeral ever held in Boone County. He also told me that they sang "It Pays to Serve Jesus" at that funeral. Dad thought that the song fit the occasion. Bobby's payoff was obvious in the respect and admiration shown by his mourners.

Not long after Bobby's death, my dad was baptized and was a faithful church member for forty years. I always felt that Bobby's service paid off for me and my family through Dad.

I didn't think much about church finances when I was attending church as a boy. The church wasn't a rich church, but the income was always adequate. If there were money problems in the church, they passed me by. Dad tithed his money, and I can remember when he earned $35.00 weekly. He gave $2.00, Mother gave $1.00, and my sister and I gave 25¢ each. I'm not sure that my family paid much attention to the way the church spent the money. They just gave it.

My hometown had about 250 people, many of them elderly people. Bob Patterson and I bought two push lawn mowers and contracted to mow yards. Most yards were worth fifty cents. I tithed the yard money. Later on I got a job for the six summers of junior and senior high school working for the county road department. We worked nine hours a day for five days and half day on Saturday for $15.00 weekly. It was a good job for a boy and I wouldn't have gotten it if my uncle hadn't been county judge. And I would have lost the job if I had goofed off. I tithed the $15.00.

After school hours I picked apples, worked with a painter, helped in a hardware store, threw sacks in a feed store, and got farm jobs. My last two years in high school I made some money writing sports stories for a newspaper. I tithed what I made. And I'm still not sure what the church did with my teenage tithe money.

When I was just out of high school, seventeen to be exact, a church invited me to be their pastor. It was a small church, twenty-two members attended the night they called me. They agreed to pay me 60 percent of the weekly offering. That day my pay was $6.40. Eventually they made it $80.00 per month.

The big question in my mind wasn't whether they would pay me $6.40 or $20.00. My big question was whether I was called of God to be a pastor. The salary didn't make much difference. I just wasn't sure if being a pastor was right for me. My plans were to go to college and study journalism. I was attracted also to law, and I was fascinated by politics. I loved to play baseball; my temper was bad; I liked the girls; weddings, funerals, and baptisms frightened me. Money just wasn't that important in my consideration of the ministry.

For more than twenty-five years my major and primary source of income has been those church offerings. I have eaten, dressed, and bought automobiles with church money.

I have paid doctors and phone bills, and have taken vacation trips with those tithes. My wife and children have lived from that church money. The church has bought my books, my Cokes, and my lawn mower. The tithers paid for my piano, my shoes, and my wristwatch.

Their voluntary contributions have been my source of livelihood. Sure, it goes into the budget and is a line item. My salary isn't a large part of the budget now. In a large church with a large budget the salaries are usually obscured and most of the people have no idea what the pastor is paid. And that's OK. It is impossible to set church salaries in any form that are agreeable to the majority of the congregation. And no one in that congregation would like to have his salary discussed in an open meeting like most congregational churches discuss salaries.

There are some pastors who do in fact collect very large salaries, are comparable to big business executives and certain professional people. But most pastors in most churches have a tough time making ends meet. If a fellow went into the pastoral ministry thinking "It Would Pay to Serve Jesus," he was soon brought back to reality.

Not that there aren't ways to make money out of the church members.

Several years ago a deacon in our church came up to me after a morning service. "I would like to put $10,000 in your hand, for your personal use. You could take your family overseas, buy a new car, invest it. Do whatever you want to," he smiled sweetly. He was a professional man with his own business. I assumed that he had as much money as anyone in our church. At least he lived like he had money. But I didn't expect him to just give me $10,000. No one has ever given me a large cash gift.

He went on to explain that he "was into" a new cosmetic development. He was trying to recruit people who would invest in the cosmetic company. They would all become wealthy in a few weeks. He and his wife wanted to share this good opportunity with their Christian friends. The money was there to be made and they wanted that money to be made by Christians who would tithe. Our church income would probably increase by $50,000 in six months if we could just get our people involved in selling mink oil cosmetics. How about that?

He wanted to use my name in promoting the sales meetings. They would like for the pastor to write some letters, attend the meetings, give them some names. And, "Oh yes, you would need to make an initial investment of $2500, but you will make $10,000 after the first meeting. If you don't have your hands on $2500 right now, I'll loan it to you if you will support the program."

Although I refused to get involved, he and his wife were successful in recruiting several church members in the pyramid selling scheme. When the attorney general finally moved in, several church members had lost substantial amounts of money. Two men lost their savings; one lost his house. They had all lost their investment. The deacon who initiated it had made more than $70,000.

Some prominent clergymen put together a company called Christian Development Association. They sold stock in the company, primarily to ministers. The pitch was: "No one in our society is as underpaid as the pastor. You have the training, you put in the hours, and the people keep you on low salaries. If you will buy stock in this Christian Company, we will invest your money wisely. You will be able to do some of the things you have always wanted to do. Your church members will never know." The directors included pastors and denominational leaders. People invested.

The company invested in businesses that went broke. They purchased property that they could not sell or rent. Eventually they purchased a bank and were indicted by the Federal Government for fraud and loaning money illegally. The investors were left with worthless stock and embarrassment.

The national media has focused on certain religious television personalities. At least three of the best-known television preachers and television churches were indicted in Federal courts for fraudulently selling church bonds and other serious money scandals. These huge churches were in fact bankrupt. One television religionist reportedly had more than one million dollars worth of jewelry, and her $250,000 a year business manager sued her for a million more as his share of her earnings.

The manager of a Christian radio station smiled when he told me that he sang "The Old Rugged Cross" all the way to the bank. He couldn't resist telling me that he lived in a $220,000 house. And there was the evangelist who came to a crusade for a "freewill" offering and who announced to the congregation the first night that it took $1500 per day, 365 days a year to keep his ministry going. That same night he told a local pastor that he would pay $40,000 a year to a "good platform man." The pastor was being paid $8,000 annually.

One of the ministerial status symbols in this generation is organizing foreign tours. The minister is the tour director and he conducts worship services in all of the holy places. This began with Holy Land tours but has been enlarged now to include Russia, Monaco, and Hong Kong. The pastor earns a free trip for each four recruits. After he recruits enough to pay for Ma and all the kids, he can earn $100 spending money for each other traveler. The clergyman rarely tells the congregation that he is enlisting people because it means money. He usually describes the trip in spiritual terms. One man described his latest tour as a visit to the missionaries in the Bahamas after three exotic nights in New Orleans. These excursions are invariably described in glowing terms as the "spiritual mountain peak" of a lifetime. All for $849!

Or you can send a donation in to your local TV station and have your name bronzed in the "Archives of Faith," a museum that Jesus will go to when he returns to rule for one thousand years. Or for your freewill gift you can get a Bible with all of the second coming passages in red, or a copy of the "Arkansas Heirs" latest record, or a copy of the preachers new book "Does 666 Mean Eighteen." Or just write for "Free Offer 192—That's 192."

You can help the evangelist buy a new tire for his $120,000 bus, or you can attend a weekend prayer retreat in the Fontainebleau for only $900, or you can help send the preacher to a crusade in the Swiss Alps during the Olympics. If all else fails, you can pay $5,000 to $15,000 and get one of the Christian celebrities to give his testimony. It just makes you feel good all over to know that a movie star, or a country singer, or a third baseman is a Christian. Or you can get a former addict, a beauty queen, or a businessman who is a millionaire. These Christian celebrities are happy to testify, or speak to the Boy Scouts, but all arrangements including fees are handled by the agency, thank you.

These same kinds of people operate in the local congregation. There are clergymen and itinerants who use the people. But there are also laymen who use laymen.

It is not uncommon for insurance agents, automobile salesmen, stocks and bond salesmen, and others to sell questionable products to other church members. These people use the church relationship as the entree for the "inside deal." Other church members entice their trusting and unsuspecting "brothers" into elaborate "get rich quick," "can't miss," "has to succeed" kind of deals. I know a widow with two children who invested her life savings into a deacon's business. The deacon left town, and the widow was left holding the debt. It is not uncommon for some church members to borrow money from others, to pass bad checks to other church members, or to ask their church friends to sign notes. One man could not qualify for a home loan, so another member bought him a house. The first man made monthly payments for more than two years only to have the house sold out from under him. He had not been paying on the house, he had been paying rent. He had been duped by a church member.

How does the church handle those kinds of people who cannot distinguish service and money? This kind of exploitation may be one of the most serious problems in the modern church. Like most church problems this is a people problem.

Most church members are like my dad. They give their money, and they have confidence in the administration of the church finances. They usually trust the pastor and the church committees and boards. There is something to be said for that kind of confidence. The average congregational church will adopt a budget and conduct regular business meetings with a very small percentage of the members present. Perhaps they just don't care. Or they may think their opinion and their vote are not important. They probably do not attend or participate in these meetings because they trust the leadership.

Most churches are open and honest in their church finance records. They publish periodic accounts of receipts and expenditures for any member of the congregation to study, question, and vote on. The typical church does not manipulate the money. Any member can be informed and involved if the members want the information and the involvement.

Financial scandal with church contributions is rare. This is a compliment to the leadership of the local congregation. There are always jokes about treasurers who run away with the offering, but these kinds of experiences are so rare that they are jokes.

This is one of the most interesting aspects of a church and her people. A congregation of people voluntarily give their money to their church. Bankers, truck drivers, schoolteachers, attorneys, widows, and salesmen mingle their offerings Sunday after Sunday. These collections of volunteer gifts amount to millions of dollars every week. No one has to give. No one has to give any amount. But they give.

Occasionally a church will get overextended and go bankrupt. Again, this is so rare that one is hard put to think of a local church that has gone bankrupt. The church may cut her ministry back. They may refinance, or relocate, or even merge with another church. They may be late paying some bills, but typically, a church operates with integrity and conscience.

The committees and boards that handle the church budget will be a representative group from the congregation. A man who earns $100 weekly may be on a church budget committee that spends $5,000 weekly. Usually these laymen use good judgement and have a deep sense of commitment. They resist the temptations to be arbitrary or secretive. They try to be open and fair.

If the local church can handle their corporate finances in an open and fair way, the itinerant religionist can do the same thing. Although the financial openness of the Billy Graham Association is not the most obvious reason for Graham's tremendous impact, it is surely one of the most important reasons for his success and his durability.

I was general chairman for a crusade with Grady Wilson in 1967 and had the same chair when Billy Graham came to Lexington for a crusade in 1971.

During those months of hard work and intensive preparation, I learned the vital importance of openness about finances. Our budget for the Wilson Crusade was $58,000 and for the Graham Crusade we needed $98,000. We worked out the local budget. We published it. We kept accurate accounts of every donation and gave receipts. We had the books audited. We published the audit. We explained from the platform prior to receiving the offering how much we needed and why. We reported the amount received to the crusade audience. When we reached our goal, we quit taking collections. All of these steps were taken with the encouragement and approval of the Billy Graham Association. The community responded favorably to this kind of stewardship.

Since those two good community crusades, other evangelists and religionists have come to town for crusades, rallies, one-night stands, and television marathons. In every case, there has been an intense hard sell for money. There has been no local control and no open accounting. Our city would not respond to this kind of secret operation. The people resented the persistent and offensive appeal for funds. Billy Graham and his local supporters are above suspicion, the modern Gantry is subject to cynical ridicule. The legitimate itinerant must be open or he should be exposed.

Church leaders have an obligation and duty to find out the facts about the religionist who is appealing for funds. If those facts are not available, then the religionist should be exposed. If we can pass a law requiring financial disclosure by elected officials, does the religionist have the moral right to operate behind a shield of secrecy?

It is my opinion that integrity and openness are the best and only answer to financial chicanery within the church. This is not to suggest that church members become suspicious muckrakers. It is to suggest that people be more responsible and honest in dealing with other church members. There isn't much chance that the church member who is swindling or ripping off other members will be persuaded to change his style. He has already decided that religious people are pigeons, and he will work that territory.

Members who have been "taken" have a responsibility to expose the rascal. They must let some judgement begin in the house of God.

We must keep a sense of balance. The charlatans are rare. They do not appear often. Most church members are scrupulously honest about their finances. They pay their tithes, their taxes, and their debts. They are jealous of their financial reputation, and they have the same feeling about their church's reputation. Church members can trust one another, and they do. This trust is what makes them vulnerable to the greedy person in their midst.

The church must also be able to help her members define greed. In every church and every city there are people who are extremely poor. The economic calamity of the past two or three years has been a terrible crisis to the aged, the unemployed, and the broken families in our society. Rising costs of food, rent, utilities, and gasoline has brought many of our people to a place of utter despair and fear. We still have the poor with us.

Big business and big labor has been dominated by the code of greed. Our capitalistic system is the best in the world, and it can withstand every pressure, except the pressure of greed. We apparently are no longer able to distinguish between a fair wage and greed. We have let greed dominate our economy while frightened politicians stand by. In all of this profound moral collapse, churchmen have been strangely silent.

This presents a serious challenge to the church. We must be honest in our preaching and teaching. More than that we must be honest and open in our financial relationships with other church members.

How do these greedy Gantrys fit into the church? If is difficult for the church to tolerate them because they are operating out of an extremely cynical attitude. Exploitation is always ugly. Exploiting sincere people in the name of religion is blasphemous. It is virtually impossible for the church to minister to those persons who use the church for financial gain.

From the time of Simon Magus until today there have been those who thought silver and gold were the keys to the kingdom. Only eternity will reveal what great harm they have done to the church. This kind of conduct may be the great scandal of the Christian faith.

But in spite of those parasites, the church people have built a consistent reputation for personal honesty and corporate integrity. The very fact that society expects church people to be honest is witness to the financial integrity of church people. The rascal is the exception to that rule.

Perhaps Peter said it best, "Thy money perish with thee."

6
"WHO CARES ANYWAY?"

When Francis Mathews made a profession of faith in a Sunday night church service, word spread rapidly through the community that Francis had been saved. Francis was not a notorious sinner. He was the youngest of five children in the Mathews family. The other four were girls, and Francis had always resented being given a girl's name.

Francis was nearly fifty when he joined the church. His parents were the pillars of the church, although it was generally understood that Mrs. Mathews was the real pillar and that Mr. Mathews never disagreed with her in any temporal or spiritual matters. The four Mathews daughters, their husbands, and their heirs were the most prominent family in the church. It was also understood that the Mathews women exacted control over their own families and the affairs of the church.

Perceptive pastors who had tried to convert Francis had realized that he resented the church like he resented the female domination of his family. He identified the church as another place where the Mathews women worked out their plans to control people. The pastor usually had some conflict with the Mathews women, and he sympathized with Francis. Consequently, no one tried very hard to get Francis into the church.

Francis had four sons and a good wife. His good wife took the little boys to church, and one by one they were baptized. Francis attended each baptism, and the night the last son was baptized Francis made a profession of faith. Everyone was shocked, including the Mathews women. His wife understood his feeling for the boys, and she wasn't surprised. Francis had always said that he "believed." It wasn't belief that kept him out of the church, his hang-up was his mother and sisters. The night of his decision Francis asked the pastor to go by and visit his neighbor. He said his neighbor needed help. The neighbor needed all the help he could get from God and the church according to Francis.

I went by the next week to see the neighbor, Fred. I drove down a narrow dusty road to a house that could be seen from the highway. I had seen the house before and had intended to visit there. The people who lived there were poor, at least the house gave signs of poverty. The floor planks were broken on the porch. The screen door was torn and hanging by one hinge. The shutters were dangling in various degrees of collapse. Everything needed paint.

I knocked twice. No one answered, but I could hear a radio. So I called out, "Anyone home?" A little, red-headed boy came running around the corner of the porch. He was about six, with ragged jeans and a face dotted with freckles. He told me to come around to the back. Said his dad was in the backyard.

Fred was sitting under a sour apple tree. A jug of beer was between his knees. He didn't have a shirt on and was barefooted. He was a big man with bright red hair matted above his sweaty face. Two pups and two or three cats were also stretched out under the tree. The backyard had an abandoned refrigerator, an abandoned washing machine and other assorted household discards, some worn farm implements, and various pieces of automobiles. A flower garden incongruously was growing in the midst of the junk. Fred had been working in the flower garden.

The visit was easy enough. He told me about his wife who worked in a bakery in town and about his four children.

Three of the children were teenagers. He worked on the railroad, when he worked. He apologized for the house and yard and said that he was going to get everything fixed up and cleaned up. I've heard drunks say that time and time again. When they are sober, or nearly sober, they are embarrassed by the neglect and disintegration of their material things.

Fred said that he had been "laying off" coming to church and he sure planned to be there Sunday. Of course sometimes the railroad called him out on Sunday, and it was possible that some of his wife's relatives might come by to visit. But if he didn't work and if no one came to visit, he would be at church. Not that he was promising, he didn't intend to promise, but he would be at church one of these days.

He did not come to church that Sunday or any Sunday for more than two years. Although Fred did not come to church, I was aware of him. His family periodically made news in our little town. Fred drank too much. There were others in the town that drank too much, but Fred's exploits were more dramatic and more repulsive to the community. So they talked.

I was a student-pastor at the time and lived two hours away on campus. Once Fred's wife called me long distance from the bakery to tell me that the fourteen-year-old daughter had been picked up for shoplifting. The next day I called the juvenile officers, and they cooperated. The girl got back in school, and she started coming to church regularly. Later that year they suspended her from school for cheating, then they expelled her for a sex adventure with six other eighth-grade pupils. The other pupils were suspended, but she was expelled.

There wasn't and isn't much employment opportunity for a fourteen-year-old girl who has been expelled from school. We couldn't find her a job, and we couldn't get her back in school. She refused to go back to school even if they would admit her. One Sunday when I got to church, one of her friends told me that she had married a fellow who was thirty-two and had moved to West Virginia. I had some conscience pangs, realizing that I had intervened on her behalf with juvenile authorities and school authorities but had never really talked to her or listened to her. I knew quite a bit about her but did not know her at all. It was an uncomfortable feeling that I handled by reminding myself that my school and church work kept me so busy. And the church was growing. More members. More money. More programs. More ministry. We were even going to build a new building. All of that takes time.

I do not know what ever happened to that girl.

The oldest boy made news. He was wild and reckless. He rode motorcycles and drove cars too fast. In a small town there is always a gang of teenagers who aggravate and intimidate the elders. The older boy was the leader of that gang. Some of the elders, like the Mathews women, called the police regularly about the boys. They felt that the boys should be run out of town.

We had a hayride for the church kids one night. The gang followed the truck for miles. When the church kids had their weiner roast, some of the kids wanted to invite the "gang" to eat. But the adult chaperones overruled them. The chaperones said that was just asking for trouble. Trouble came when the gang rode their motorcycles through the prayer circle around the campfire right in the midst of "Jacob's Ladder." The kids scattered to the truck, and the devotional was never given.

Fred's oldest boy wracked up his motorcycle and broke his leg. I visited him in the hospital. He told me that he was going to join the Army. The last I heard he was making a career out of the Army.

The oldest girl got pregnant when she was sixteen. It stirred up the community because she said one of the Mathews descendants was the father of the child. The Mathews family was ready to go to court. Fred didn't have the money for a trial, but he was determined that the baby would have a name. The oldest daughter came to me and told me that the Mathews heir was the father but she had had sex with other boys and she knew that they would embarrass her. She said her dad didn't have any money and besides, "He will probably get drunk the day of the trial." I told her I would try to find a home for unwed mothers.

The very next day she ran off with Toby Heringer, and they got married in Tennessee. Toby was an eighteen-year-old school dropout who worked on a farm owned by the Mathews. The marriage worked, and they still live in Tennessee.

After the oldest daughter and Toby left, Fred's wife left him. She took the little boy, and they moved to the town where she worked in the bakery. Fred was alone.

It was past midnight when I got the phone call from the county police chief. I was in school ninety long miles from the church. The police chief told me that Fred had gone berserk. He had barricaded himself in the barn behind his house. He had guns and beer. Francis Mathews had discovered him, and Fred had shot at Francis. In fact, he was shooting at anyone who went into the lot around the barn. The police were there, had been there for four or five hours. They didn't want to shoot Fred or burn the barn. They had tried to entice him out of the barn.

Fred told them that he wanted to talk to me. He said he would come out of the barn if I would take him to the hospital.

The police chief thought it was worth the risk if I was willing to try it. I explained that it would take me at least two hours to get there. And I told him that I didn't know Fred very well, in fact I had only met him once in his backyard under a sour apple tree.

When I arrived at Fred's place, it looked like a movie set. Police cars, an ambulance, spotlights blazing against the barn from every direction. A crowd of people held back by the police. I saw a lot of familiar church faces in that crowd. Everyone was gray in the reflection of the spotlights. People like the Mathews were mad. I was frightened.

They gave me a speaker to talk through and I walked out, alone, into the pool of light in the barnyard. Fred could see me, I knew. I called to him and in a few moments, that seemed forever, he came out the barn door. He threw down the guns and walked quietly to me. He was sobbing.

It was a long night. I stayed with him on the ride to the police station. Later he was sent to a secure ward in a large mental hospital. For weeks after that night, I visited Fred in the hospital. He had treatment, counseling, and eventually an operation. Through it all I stuck with him. We became friends.

When he was allowed to come home, he immediately joined the church and was baptized. When the church door was open, Fred was there. He began to sing in the choir. He helped around the church building, caring for the yard, painting, repairing the broken things. He planted a flower garden on the front lawn of the church. It was a lovely flower garden.

He fixed up his house. He painted the house, cleaned the junk out of the yard, and repaired the front porch. It looked like it did when he first moved there twenty years before with his young wife.

During his hospitalization and his recovery Fred never heard one word from his wife and the youngest boy. She had married again and apparently was happy in that second marriage. The two older children came by to see Fred on rare occasions. He did not seem to be depressed by his family's unconcern. He did not talk about them much.

The people in the church were slow to accept Fred. They did not ignore him, nor did they criticize him. They were reluctant to warm up to Fred. They were polite, they complimented his flower garden on the church lawn, they thanked him for the repair work he did on the building.

They accepted him in the choir. I felt that Fred was isolated by the people—they had drawn an invisible circle around him.

One day Fred was working at the church and he asked me if I remembered the first day that we had met. I did remember.

He said: "I used to see you drive by the house. Even when I was drinking heavy I would recognize your car. I thought you would stop by and talk to me again. You knew about my problems with my kids. You knew about my wife leaving me. You knew that I was drinking too much.

"Why didn't you ever stop again?

"Didn't you care?"

I didn't answer Fred's question. It was an accusation. It is an accusation that always haunts me. It is too similar to the good Samaritan story and those who pass by on the other side in our generation. Far too often we rush by the people like Fred who have broken homes, broken minds, and broken hearts. We care, but we obviously don't care enough.

Fred did fine for more than two years. He was faithful and dependable in church. He went back to work on the railroad. He didn't drink at all for more than two years. We learned to expect Fred's acceptable behavior. He seemed to be stable and happy.

More than once I had heard rumors that he was drinking again during that third year. Then he began missing some church services. I stopped by the house and immediately noticed that it was not as neat as it was on my last visit. He wasn't drinking, at least it wasn't apparent to me. He was surly and said that the church people weren't all that I thought they were. He said that they were hard on him about booze, but some of the church people drank more than he ever had.

Fred rarely attended church by the end of the third year and was drinking in public again. My last visit with him was tragic. Fred was extremely sick. He was convinced that he had uncovered a Communist plot in the little elementary school. Those same Communist conspirators had gotten into the church. He had quit the railroad job because the Communists were in control there, too. Without his job, he was living in poverty. Hungry. Filthy. Suspicious. Drinking bootleg liquor. Terribly sick. Fascinated by television and his conversation about Communist plots.

I called some social workers, and they had Fred committed to a large mental hospital. The treatment this time was not successful. His physical and mental condition deteriorated. Eventually I quit visiting him because he did not know me and did not respond to my visits in any way. The doctors do not expect any improvement in Fred's condition. The prognosis is grim.

Every evangelical church has someone like Fred in their membership. Someone like Fred who lives under the influence of the church. Someone like Fred who challenges the outreach and caring ministry of that church. Their family life and their personal life deteriorates. They are miserable, and the church seems designed to do something for them. The church looks like the best, the only, hope for these kinds of persons. But often the church seems impotent.

Did the church fail in the beginning with Fred? For a variety of reasons the church had not reached his children in the Sunday School and the youth programs. Perhaps the entree to Fred's family was through the children when they were small. At that time Fred was not drinking as much, his marriage was stronger than it would be later, and he had the responsibility of the children. Maybe the church failed with the children because of neglect or perhaps there was a subtle prejudice against Fred's children because they were poor.

Or perhaps the ministry of the church to families was and is inadequate. The traditional Sunday School and worship program may not be enough for a family like Fred's troubled family. Our church programs have been designed for reasonably stable families and stable people. We have been perplexed by and frightened of the troubled families. The fractured family is out of place in the program designed for the stable family. Even if Fred and his disturbed family had attended our church with their profound problems, they might have left with their peculiar needs unmet.

Maybe Fred was right. Maybe the pastor and the people simply did not come enough. This kind of accusation can be written in tall letters over any church door. "Don't You Care?" Whatever else our Christian discipleship involves, it must involve caring about people. Whatever else our church program involves, it must involve caring for people. Anyone has a right to ask Fred's question, "Do You Care?" And the church must constantly answer affirmatively. The church must care or the church ceases to be the church.

To be Christian is to care. That is easier said than done. Some people are resistant to your caring. They resent it. Some people successfully mask their needs and cover their fears. They play games. They live distorted lives, and we are not sensitive to their needs because of the camouflage.

With people like Fred, caring is difficult because the problems seem so complex. The successive scrapes that his children became involved in are serious and frustrating. How do you help? Perhaps the church is not equipped to handle juvenile delinquents, alcoholics, mentally ill persons. Our society does not expect the church to deal effectively with these kinds of people. We have a proliferation of governmental and private agencies that try to help people with these problems.

Government has spent multiplied millions in these rehabilitation and recovery programs. They do extensive research. They staff their programs with well-trained people. In some places they expect the church to be a partner, albeit a junior partner, in the program. Most of the time in most places the church is ignored.

It is easy to care for Fred's "spiritual life" in the church and let the secular agencies deal with his disintegrated marriage, his troubled kids, his booze problem, and his mental illness. Fred and his family may be beyond the competence of the church. His problems may be a legitimate concern of the government like national defense, the fire department, and highway building are the legitimate concerns of the government. But it is not possible to separate his "spiritual life" from his family, his drinking, or his mental health.

But the church people did ignore Fred prior to his dramatic breakdown and the bizarre event in the barn. After his return from the hospital and his baptism, the church people were not comfortable with him. They tolerated him, but they did not accept him. Their conversation with Fred was just small talk. They did not seriously consider electing Fred to any of the church offices. They did not invite him into their homes for a meal or a visit.

He made them uncomfortable. He was divorced and did not have contact with his children, and most of the church members talked most about their family. He had been in a mental hospital; he was an alcoholic; he had created a community furor with his guns. He was not educated, didn't read, and had little interest in current events. There wasn't much to talk with Fred about. And he was shy and withdrawn. He would not initiate any conversation or involvement. If he was sensitive to his isolation and aloneness, he did not indicate it. After all, he kept attending church.

For generations people like Fred have had dramatic conversion experiences that have changed everything. They literally behave like new creatures. Their personality changes in an uncanny way. They become attractive, self-confident, and verbal. They say that they are never tempted to drink again. Their befuddled minds become clear. Their embarrassing past is all forgotten, except when they give their testimony. Their associates in the "old days" do not recognize them, and they marvel at the change conversion brings. This happens often enough to encourage us all to believe that it can happen.

No experienced Christian thinks it will happen that way every time. We have seen too many who were sincere in their decision who falter and fail, who go forward one step and regress two. We have seen alcoholics stay dry for months only to plunge into a spectacular drunk. We have seen deacons and clergymen go morally bankrupt and emotionally chaotic. We have seen relatives and dear friends who have made a conscientious effort at discipleship slip back into the old ways. Or even into new ways that are more immature and immoral than the behavior of the past. It is not peculiar to Fred.

Maybe it's the genes. Maybe they are just born to fail, born to lose. Maybe there are things in their person that are just beyond the church. In another age people believed that "blood would tell." They believed that folks inherited certain traits from their parents and grandparents. They believed that some people were "born to sin" or "born to virtue."

Although that idea is not fashionable in this generation, there is still some of it in our thought patterns. And with reason. This perplexes the churchman who believes that conversion and a loving ministry will always produce change in a man. Then someone like Fred comes along and accepts the conversion ministry route and still regresses into his old ways.

Others rationalize a man like Fred in theological jargon. Some would say that he was predestined to his broken life and that no power on earth can change his destiny. This adds the weight of heaven's predetermination to the idea of "blood will tell." Those who reject that kind of theology dismiss Fred and his kind by saying that they just "weren't ever saved." If Fred had been honestly converted, he would never have backslidden. He simply did not trust Jesus with all of his heart. They say that if Fred had really been saved he would not have backslidden.

And when all of the explanations have been given and all of the frustrations expressed, the church still has Fred and his kind. We did not do all that we could have done for Fred, but we did something. We did not lead him to a complete new life, but he did have a few good years. Our help was apparently inadequate, but we did help. Our caring was fragile and fumbling, but we did care.

The church obviously did not meet the need for Fred and his family, but we tried. And at times that is all we can do.

7
THE DROPOUT

Ordained men leave the ministry. The church struggles with the twin problem of declining seminary enrollments and the dropouts. These twins have left many churches without pastors and have created a sense of urgency in all denominations about ministerial recruitment.

More than one hundred thousand ordained men left the ministry during the last decade. They teach school, sell insurance, work for the government, go back to college, and find employment in a variety of ways. Their seminary training does not prepare them for other jobs, and they are hard put to find work.

Richard Charles had been a member of our church two or three months before I knew that he was a dropout. He had been graduated from one of the large prestige seminaries that our denomination owns and operates. During his seminary days Richard had been pastor of a rural church and shortly after graduation had been employed in a countyseat town church. He dropped out while in the countyseat town and moved to the city. He was working as a private detective.

Richard was a handsome young man. He was about six feet tall, well dressed, premature gray hair. He seemed shy and self-conscious. His wife, Chris, had joined the church the same Sunday, but she had been back to church only once. She was a doll. Vivacious. Pretty. No one could ignore Chris. She comes on strong.

They were both from Georgia. He grew up in a small

town in southwest Georgia. His parents were church members, although his father didn't attend church often. There were five boys in the family. Richard was in the middle, two older and two younger. The boys were like the old man. They worked hard on the farm, fished, hunted, and went to movies and dances on the weekend. Richard did his share of the work, the old man didn't allow any of them privileges. But Richard was different; he read. He enjoyed being alone. He would rather walk in the woods than hunt in the woods.

He was a conscientious student in high school. The other boys were dropouts. He played baseball and football, the other boys weren't interested in team sports. Richard wanted to go to college. The other boys got jobs as soon as they could legally quit school. The old man used to say that Richard was so different, he sometimes wondered if Richard was his. The old man also said that Richard could go to college, but he would have to pay his own way.

The old man was not Richard's hero. Richard always had mixed feelings about the old man. This still worried him. The old man wrecked his pick-up truck and was killed instantly when Richard was pastor in the countyseat town. Richard was sorry. He felt a loss. He ached for his mother and was impotent in consoling the other brothers who grieved excessively. But for some reason, or reasons, Richard didn't grieve. He didn't weep. The old man and Richard didn't understand one another.

Richard's hero was Dr. Mayo, the Bible professor at the Baptist college, who preached at Richard's church. Not that Dr. Mayo was the regular pastor. But every time a pastor would leave the church, they would employ Dr. Mayo as interim pastor. Often these interims would last three or four months.

It was during one such interim when Richard was eleven that Dr. Mayo baptized him. It was during a similar interim when Richard was fifteen that he decided to go to college.

This was reaffirmed when Dr. Mayo returned to the church for three months during Richard's last year in high school.

Dr. Mayo was well educated. He had a splendid vocabulary. He wore attractive clothes and drove a new car. He was witty and pleasant. He was a good listener and an excellent public speaker. You could talk to him and know that he understood. When he talked to you, he spoke quietly but firmly. He made sense to Richard. The old man and most of the other people in town talked all of the time, but they didn't make sense. Their conversation was loud, incessant, usually vulgar, and it seemed to Richard, always pointless.

Richard felt that a man like Dr. Mayo made a difference. What he thought made a difference. His opinions made a difference. People would respect and listen to Dr. Mayo. About this time Richard decided that he wanted to make a difference, too. He wanted to turn people around, give them direction, help them. Dr. Mayo was doing that because he was educated and because he was a man of God.

The church had always talked about a God-called-ministry. God chose his spokesmen. He selected Moses and Amos. He picked out the prophets, apostles, and saints of every century. If he chose you, he would give you power and persuasion. If he chose you, he would provide the opportunity. He would never leave you nor forsake you. The apostle Paul believed that he had been chosen before he was born. Jeremiah believed the same. So did Richard. That's why he was different. God had selected him from birth to be a prophet. He was one of the chosen, and he would help turn the world around.

College and seminary followed. Seven tough years of study. He worked at secular jobs to pay the bills: pumping gas, assembly line, school bus driver, house painter, male nurse, YMCA director, basketball referee. His grades were about average, and he accumulated knowledge. He wasn't the brightest boy in the class, but no one was more eager to learn. Richard was a pleasure to his teachers. They predicted that he would become an influential pastor. He had the credentials.

But he is a dropout at twenty-eight and unhappily employed as a private detective.

The public assumes that ministerial dropouts have been forced out. Many of them are. Some of them get into moral scrapes, women usually. The Roman Catholics won't tolerate a married priest, Protestants won't tolerate a promiscuous pastor. A pastor can be ruined in his work by a real or implied indiscretion with a woman. Elmer Gantry isn't dead, and there is enough sex scandal in the ministry for more novels of the nonfiction type.

Some pastors don't pay their bills. Or they write bad checks. Or borrow from their members and don't pay the debt. Some dropouts get hooked on booze and become alcoholics. Or they manipulate people and get fired by an angry congregation. Some of them gossip and lie. They may get into trouble because of their wife or children. There are many reasons that men are forced out of the ministry.

They didn't force Richard though, he quit. Richard quit because he could not change people. The members of his church were kind to him. They paid him well. They provided a decent house for him to live in. They sincerely liked his wife and treated her with open respect. They did not meddle in his personal life, in fact he had an enormous amount of freedom to set his own pace and plan his schedule. The church respected him as a man, and they traditionally honored the role of their pastor.

He was always welcome in their homes. They were grateful when he visited them in their illnesses and sorrows. They complimented his sermons. They invited him to the Kiwanis Club, the family reunions, and to ball games. He was intimately involved with them at birth, death, wedding, and crisis. He was a part of their life. But he didn't see much change in them that could be attributed to his influence.

Richard quit because he thought that church people reflected their culture and that their church was a part of that culture. He felt that the church should be the light of the world, salt of the earth, the leaven in the lump. He thought that church people should go against the grain of society. They should rebel. Their convictions should set them apart.

There were an accumulation of things that pushed Richard out of the ministry. The people were harsh in their criticism of divorce. They gossiped about divorced people. Richard thought they should be compassionate. They pointed out to him that divorced people attended church and held some church offices, but Richard said they were patronizing to the divorced.

Richard wanted the church to integrate. There weren't many blacks in the countyseat town, and they did have their own church. There was a spirited debate in the church about bringing black children to Vacation Bible School, but the church did vote to integrate the Vacation Bible School. Again Richard felt like the people retained their prejudices and that they were patronizing to the black children.

Although churches traditionally delivered Christmas and Thanksgiving baskets to the poor, they had no deep concern about housing, unemployment, the handicapped, and education. If there was a fire the people would collect food, and clothing, and furniture for the victims. They would take food to a home where there was a death in the family. Some of Richard's most active members were insensitive to poverty, and his sermons did not change their views. Some of his members oppressed the poor and had no conscience about it.

The people could get excited about the church budget, but were disinterested in welfare. They would argue about what color to paint a Sunday School room in the church, but gave no thought to a family of four living in a two-room apartment. They would collect money to send missionaries to Africa, but would argue about accepting an Afro-American into their church. They would seek election to offices in the church, but would insist that politics should be kept out of the church.

That disgusted Richard. He was convinced that they would never change.

He became an outspoken critic of the Vietnam war. He tried to be against all war. Veterans of World War II told him that he should have been alive then. If they hadn't fought and won that war, Hitler and the Japs would have run the world. One deacon had lost a son in Vietnam. He became so angry with Richard that he quit the church. Richard tried to explain to him that he respected the dead soldier and all men who did their duty.

Richard wanted the people in his church to be against the war because they were Christians. He said that the young men in the church should refuse to go. He said that the boys who went to Canada and Sweden were the real heroes.

The church didn't fire him. The deacons advised him to quit preaching about politics. The men weren't mad at him at that deacons' meeting, in fact a couple of them asked him to go to the university football game with them. The meeting broke up with everyone in good humor.

Richard realized that night that they weren't angry because they knew what he said and what he believed really didn't make that much difference.

So he quit.

The people were surprised. They said he was one of the best preachers they had ever had. They said that Richard really was getting to the teenagers.

Richard said that he joined our church because he hadn't given up on the church; he had given up on himself.

Most churches have someone on the membership roll who has been a full-time church worker at some time. Many of these men left the vocational ministry because they, like

Richard, could not get people to change. They still feel some loyalty and obligation to the church, so they do join another church.

For every disillusioned former clergyman, there are a thousand disillusioned church members, especially young people. It is true that our churches and our people fall far short of the teachings of Jesus. We are tied up with machinery and the church moves or changes slowly, if at all.

And for all of our lip service to the ideals of the kingdom of God, we seem intent on building religious empires out of budgets, buildings, and new buses. There are a lot of material things in any church program. Things that are counted, measured, weighed, bought, and tasted. It is difficult to equate this kind of empire with the kingdom of God.

Hypocrisy? Yes, that is in the church, too. Members who behave in an inconsistent and shocking manner. Everything Richard found in his church can be found in any church. People do have pride and arrogance. They are prejudiced and judgmental. They are self-serving and arbitrary in their kind deeds.

We have been dishonest in our presentation of the church. We have promised too much. We have said things about the church that are simply not true, at least they are not true all of the time. We have been unwilling to confess our sins and our limitations. We have been terribly self-conscious about our humanity. The church has role-played a distorted image. This distortion has made disillusion and rejection inevitable.

Our only hope is integrity. The church must admit her weakness and limitation. We can save young men like Richard by telling them that there is always the limitation and the distortion of our sinful humanity. The church has not attained. It is not a collection of saints. It has not and will not gain perfection. There are always failures and frustrations. The answer to our humanity is an honest admission of our weakness.

8
AUNT MAMIE'S PIANO

The church building was small; there were about 110 theatre-type seats. Some of them, five to be exact, were broken and couldn't be used. There was one seat on the left with a ragged edge, and Mrs. Hollis had torn her stockings on it last Sunday. Really the one with the ragged edge shouldn't be counted as useable, so that left 104 seats.

It was a frame building painted white, but the paint was chipping. No stained-glass windows, just tall windows like you might see in an old house. There was a bell tower, but the bell didn't ring. There wasn't a rope to the bell anyway. They said that an old cat had kittens in the bell tower. They didn't like to have kittens in the bell tower, but the cat did keep the birds out of the tower. Old man Schnieder lived across the street, and he complained about the bell, so they quit ringing it.

There were wires across the interior of the church. Drapes hung on the wires, and they could be pulled together to divide the room into Sunday School rooms. The drapes were green. The drape partitions made six classrooms in the auditorium. The ladies had made the drapes.

The pulpit was elevated about twelve inches off the floor. The pulpit stand was a box-like lectern. It was wide enough to hide the preacher's body. Behind the pulpit stand there was a framed painting of Jesus on the cross. The picture invariably hung crooked. It always tipped to the left. There were two dining room chairs on the platform for the singer and preacher.

In front of the pulpit there was a communion table. It was similar to a coffee table, only taller than the average coffee table. There was a green linen scarf on the table. The green scarf matched the color of the Sunday School drapes.

The walls were also green. They were painted regularly. The men did the painting. Spots of green paint were on the seats. Each year the church voted to buy the paint, and the men painted the walls. Last year Tom Barnett wanted to paint the walls and seats white. He thought white was more religious than green. The other men said that it would take too much paint if they changed colors. Besides the women didn't want green drapes with white walls.

Tom decided that white would be bad because of the stoves. The church had two old fashioned potbellied stoves, one to each side of the platform. No one in the church had stoves in their homes; Mr. McNeil had been the last member to get a furnace. They figured that they didn't use the church but once or twice a week and a furnace would cost too much. Mr. McNeil always donated the coal, and he was dependable about building the fires every Sunday and for weddings and funerals. Mrs. Hollis thought that the old-time stoves were conducive to the old-time religion.

Most of the furniture in the building had been donated by some member, or by some group in the church. Some large and wealthy churches put up plaques to identify the donors. These church members didn't approve of plaques. They didn't need them. Nearly everyone knew who paid for the drapes, the paint, the stoves, the picture of Jesus, the communion table. They knew who gave the chairs on the platform. It wasn't necessary to give credit or put up bronze plaques. Mr. McNeil bought the coal and had donated a stove. Things like this were understood.

But Aunt Mamie's piano was a problem. No one talked much about it, but it was a problem. The church had always had a piano, and Gerry Strong played it well. Gerry played by ear and had played for church since she was eleven. Gerry had a beat. Tom Barnett led the singing, and he often said that no one in the county could play gospel music like Gerry. And you could count on Gerry: When the door was open, Gerry was there. There wasn't a song that Gerry couldn't play. Just hum it or whistle it and Gerry would play it.

Gerry did jazz up the music. No doubt about that. She played with a lot of feeling. The church didn't have a lot of fine things like the big churches, but they had peppy and enthusiastic singing. Gerry enjoyed it.

It wasn't so much that Aunt Mamie didn't like Gerry. She did like Gerry. But Aunt Mamie didn't like jazzy music. She didn't like gospel music. She thought it was disrespectful and sacrilegious. She didn't think that the Lord would be pleased with a lot of foot-patting singing. Aunt Mamie couldn't imagine an angel choir praising the Lord in heaven with some hillbilly song that sounded like a square dance.

Aunt Mamie was respected in the church. She was old, very old. No one knew how old, because she never told. Mrs. Hollis could remember back in horse and buggy days that Aunt Mamie came to church in a carriage. Mrs. Hollis's father drove a jolt wagon to church. Aunt Mamie had the only carriage. She seemed old even then.

Some people said she was a widow. Others said that she had never been married but had been in love, and her lover had died. Others thought that she had been jilted. Anyhow, she lived alone in a modest house. People said that she served tea when she had guests from the countyseat. No one in the church ever visited in her home except the pastors, and they always went by invitation only.

Aunt Mamie attended church every Sunday morning. She always made a donation twice a year. Her donation was the largest gift that the church received. She never came to Sunday School. She never sang. She wasn't friendly but was always polite. Tom Barnett said she was a "proper lady." Tom used to tell Gerry that someday he was going to get Aunt Mamie to sing. Tom took pride in getting everyone to sing. He gave up though on Aunt Mamie.

One Sunday morning everyone was shocked when they got to Sunday School to see a sparkling, brand-new Baldwin piano sitting on the left side of the pulpit. It was a beauty! Tom couldn't wait to tell Gerry. The old piano was in bad shape. Tom tried to open it. It was locked. People stood around and looked at the new piano. The kids rubbed the shiny finish. But it was locked.

During Sunday School the pastor told Tom and Gerry that Aunt Mamie had donated the piano. It wasn't to be opened or played without her permission. It was not to be used for gospel music. Nothing personal, but Gerry wasn't to play it.

Aunt Mamie hoped that some time they could arrange for a pianist to come and play religious music—moving music. Music that would provoke worship and praise to God. Music that required artistry more than rhythm. Music that was in good taste. These were Aunt Mamie's hopes and aspirations. For this reason she had bought the piano.

She would keep the key.

If no one ever came to the church who could and would play the new piano to Aunt Mamie's satisfaction, then it would not be played until her funeral. In that case the church was to secure the services of Mrs. Woodmont who was organist at the Episcopal church in the countyseat. Mrs. Woodmont already had the list of songs that Aunt Mamie wanted at her funeral.

Within a week everyone in the church knew the story of Aunt Mamie's piano.

So the piano sits to the left of the pulpit. It has never been unlocked. It has never been played. It is no longer shining nor mysterious. Even the little children call it Aunt Mamie's piano.

Aunt Mamie comes to church every Sunday. She doesn't sing. Gerry always stops by and speaks to Aunt Mamie. It's no big issue in the church. When a new preacher comes to the church, Aunt Mamie always tells him about the piano. Tom dropped some green paint on the piano last year, but he cleaned it off.

Aunt Mamie may live longer than Mrs. Woodmont, but Tom figures that she already has someone else briefed about her funeral music.

Every church has someone like Aunt Mamie and some relic like her piano. There are always church members who make specific donations to the building. Usually there are some strings attached. The gifts are encumbered. They are not really gifts but a kind of investment with conditions.

For centuries churches have adjusted to these donors and their donations. Who wants to question Aunt Mamie's motives? Perhaps she has the right to pick and choose her taste in church music. Perhaps she has the right to designate the purpose and object of her donation.

Eccentric? Are people who choose to live alone and maintain their own privacy eccentric? They appear eccentric and mysterious to gregarious people. A minority person seems discordant in church where the majority reach a compatible consensus.

This church is to be complimented for accepting Aunt Mamie on her own terms. They don't really understand her. They tried to make her like their songs, but she didn't like their songs. They have kept her piano closed. They will be intensely interested when it is opened for Mrs. Woodmont to play at the funeral. They clean the green paint spots off the piano. They call it Aunt Mamie's piano.

After she has died, they will leave the piano there. It may never be played again. But they won't move it for a generation or more. They will tell their children about the piano. Someday they will build a new church and the piano may be discarded then, like the bell in the bell tower.

But they will not do this quickly or casually. Church people will respect Aunt Mamie's piano. They don't quite understand, but it was a donation. And she is a church member. That makes a lot of difference to other church members.

The entire question of giving to the church is perplexing. Churches are supported by the voluntary contributions of members and friends. No one has to give money or materials. Few if any churches make giving a prerequisite for church membership. Few, if any, churches exclude members who do not give. For the most part giving has been left to the individual member and his conscience.

Not that the church has been timid in conducting fund drives and budget promotion. Churchmen have taught and preached about tithing. There are elaborate programs directed to encourage people to give and give regularly. There are many professional organizations that do nothing but guide churches in fund raising.

Collecting money is the most persistent challenge for any pastor. It is always difficult to persuade people to give enough and to give regularly. It may be equally difficult to get a unified budget adopted by the church, for all of the causes do not have equal appeal to the members.

Aunt Mamie's piano illustrates at once the genius and the agony of church giving. If everyone in the church was to pick and choose their own favorite cause, there would be no budget. If this kind of designation became a pattern, a church might have an auditorium full of pianos and no money for the electric bill. At the same time the church must acknowledge that Aunt Mamie, or anyone else, has the right to do with their own money what they choose. Even if their choice is strange.

As long as the church lives on volunteer giving, the church will confront questions like Aunt Mamie's piano.

9
"SIN IS SIN"

The first time I met Almond he told me: "Some people will say that I'm ole fashioned and out of date. Well, it may be old fashioned to stand up for what's right and to fight against the wrong. My father always told me that it is easier to do the right than it was to fight the wrong. Let me tell you something, Preacher, when it's wrong I know it. When it's wrong, I'm agin in. When it's wrong, I call it wrong."

Almond didn't give me time to reply. He shifted in his straight back chair and continued: "The trouble with the church today is right at that point. We ain't strong against sin like we should be. Time was when the church could be counted on in the battle of right and wrong. Ain't that way now. Church people lives like and acts just like the world. Can't tell them apart any more."

I went to see Almond because he had missed church for two weeks, my first two weeks in the church. Several people had described him as a pillar of the church. He had some chronic kidney problems and would never miss church services unless he was sick. So I dropped by his house for a get-acquainted visit.

"Don't know what they're teaching preachers at the seminary anymore. I always call it the cemetery myself, reckon they have killed more good preachers than they've helped. Anyhow, the last three or four from the seminary that I've heard preach are mighty weak on sin. Strong on love, but weak on sin.

"Now you take all this business about relative sin. I guess I've got as many relatives that sin as the next one," Almond chuckled and waited for my approval of his humor, "anyhow sin ain't relative. Sin is black. Sin is wrong. Sin is sin. It ain't relative. It don't depend upon who is sinning, or why they're sinning, or who else is sinning. If it was sin a hundred years ago, or ten years ago, or ten days ago, it's sinning today. The Bible is plain about that. The Lord God don't change. The Commandments don't change. Sin don't change.

"Anyhow, girls come to church in short dresses. Dresses been getting shorter and shorter. Women wearing short pants. Why, I told the deacons ten years ago that we would end up here with some deacon's wife, or worse, some preacher's wife." He stopped and looked hard at me, "Hope your wife ain't running around showing her legs that way."

"As a matter of fact, Almond."

He interrupted and continued: "Bad enough those shorts. Girls wore those things on a hayride they had for the young people. Then people keep yelling about those girls getting raped and having babies before they get married. Can't tempt a boy like that, going around with your legs showing, and not expect something to happen. I tried to get the deacons to pass a rule about how girls dress in church and on these socials. But they couldn't pass no rules, their own wives are going around half-dressed.

"Well, I did my best to fight it. Then all of the women start wearing short dresses. Wearing them to church, too. That caused me to vote for choir robes, although I don't think Baptists ought to wear robes. Too much like Catholics for me. But robes beats them short dresses. I told Fred Glass, he was choir leader, that those women in the choir ought to be in a burlesque show. Fred talked to the preacher, and they agreed that they shouldn't try to tell people how to dress. Anyhow, I'm not telling anyone how to dress, I'm saying it's a sin to be half-dressed in public. Especially in church. Follow me?

"Well I brought it up at the business meeting. I ain't sneaky. I told Fred Glass to tell that half-dressed bunch of chorus girls on the front row of the choir that I was going to. Anyhow, I made a motion that they either wear choir robes or dresses that come to their knees.

"One little imp, about eighteen years old she was, said that them short dresses were in style. Everyone was doing it. I told her that everyone might be goin to hell on a sleigh ride, too but that didn't mean the church ought to sanction or approve the sleigh ride. That shut her up.

"I'll tell you something, preacher. You know who got them to vote me down. Susan Simmons. Yes sir, Susan Simmons, the wife of a deacon. Why Susan Simmons is forty years old if she is a day. I reckon that surprises you, 'cause she sure don't look it. But both of her kids are teenagers. And I'll admit that Susan Simmons is about the best-looking woman in the church. She is one of the best-looking women I know. There ain't no reason for a woman that good looking to be showing herself to every Tom, Dick, and Harry by wearing short dresses. I can't imagine Bill Simmons letting his wife dress that way. I sure wouldn't if I was in his place.

"Susan Simmons said that she didn't think what a person wore was as important as what they were. She said that styles did change. And that people did try to dress in style. She said that I wasn't dressed exactly like Abraham Lincoln. Or George Washington. Or Jesus. I asked her if she knew how Jesus dressed. She said she didn't figure he dressed like I was.

"Then she really said something, Preacher, that I didn't think I'd hear in church. She said to me, 'Almond, if my short dress is giving you evil thoughts, I reckon you'd have evil thoughts if I was wrapped up in a blanket.' Then as if she hadn't gone too far, she said, 'Almond, you could wear your underwear to church and I wouldn't entertain one moment of lust for your body.' That's exactly what she said, Preacher. Exactly. I was so mad and so embarrassed for her ignorance and sin that I walked out before they even voted.

"Can you imagine? Right in church? A deacon's wife? A pretty, intelligent woman saying something like that? See what I mean, Preacher, the church has gotten too easy on sin.

"Now don't get me wrong. There are a lot of other sins besides shorts and mini dresses. Drinking is sin, and America is drinking to her doom. You hear a lot of people blaming Roosevelt. Wasn't up to him to keep people from drinking. It's up to the churches. Roosevelt was a good president. Prohibition just didn't work. It ain't the government's job, it's up to the people. You can't make laws and make people quit sinning.

"Cussing is sinful. How long has it been since I heard a strong sermon against cussing? Lord, I can't remember when I heard a good strong sermon about cussing. Preachers don't preach about cussing any more often than they preach about hell. Say, I hope you've got a good sermon on hell.

"You know when I was a boy, Christians took a stand against dancing and movies, too. Yes sir, people could tell that you were a Christian because you didn't dance. Want to know something? Let me tell you something about dancing.

"At one time Susan Simmons, she was Susan Nix then, and I were sweethearts. It wasn't any puppy love then either. We was seniors in high school. Everyone thought we was the perfect couple. That was back in the county before either of us moved to town. Well, we did a lot of planning about getting married after I did a couple of years in the service.

"Brother, my witness for the Lord never wavered while I was in the army. The fellows shot dice and played cards, but I wasn't tempted. They cussed and told onery jokes, but I wasn't tempted. They went to dances and picture shows, but I didn't go with them. Sure, they joked me. Made fun of me, laughed at me. But there wasn't no way that I would sin. No way.

"All that time Susan was writing me love letters. Saying that she was waiting for me. Loved me. Said we was going to get married. I believed her. Believed every word. Not one time did I sin against that girl. Not once!

"Then my momma wrote me that Susan was going to dances. She wasn't going with any one fellow. Supposed to be going with her sister. Acting as a chaperone, Momma said. I knew right then that Susan was dancing with other men. If she hadn't of been dancing with other men, she would have told me. Course she knew that dancing was sin. She knew how strong I was about sin.

"Well, don't ever underestimate sin, Preacher. When I wrote Susan and told her that Momma had told me about the dancing, I also told her to repent to God and that if she would promise not to sin like that anymore, that I would forgive her, too. Anyhow, I was in Germany, and letters was the only way I could get to her.

"Sin is strong, preacher. Sin had Susan. She would rather kept on sinning than quit. So she quit me. Broke it all up over dancing. Well, that was a long time ago. She and I just happened to end up in the same church here a few years ago. I reckon she's happy with Bill. She acts like it. Bill's a pretty good man, but he can't control Susan. Reckon it would take a strong man to control Susan.

"But you see the point, Preacher. One sin leads to another. Dancing. Swimming together. Picture shows. Short dresses. Lust. Adultery.

"I've often figured that a strong preacher could have kept Susan straight. Back when she started dancing I wrote to the preacher we had then, and I told him to preach a strong sermon about dancing. He didn't do it. And they don't preach like that now days either.

"Well, God bless you, Preacher. Appreciate you coming by to see me. My kidneys will be better in a few days.

I'll be back in church. When you're right, I'll be behind you. When you're wrong, I'll tell you so. Yes sir, I'll tell you. There ain't no point in beating around the bush about sin."

It was all true. Everything Almond told me that first time years ago was true. He does speak out about his convictions. He does think that he knows right from wrong. He is outspoken and honest. We get along. Occasionally I look out at Almond and wonder if he is really as lonely as he appears to be. Occasionally I see him looking at Susan Simmons in the choir. Wonder what Almond is thinking?

Every church has someone like Almond. They may be the most difficult people in the church to love. They are legalists pure and simple. They offend people with their self-righteousness and their legalism. They seem to enjoy putting people down and offending people. They are the ones who project the image of absolute and unquestioned moral authority. These rigid legalists are modern-day Pharisees who circle in the saints and circle out the sinners. They draw the circles, and they pass the judgements.

The legalist breeds contention and controversy in the church. They harass the pastor, and they irritate the young. Their air of moral superiority is nearly frightening at times and is always discomforting. A church must be extremely strong and patient to include a man like Almond.

But there is a trap in this situation. It is as easy for the tolerant, liberal churchmen to condemn and exclude Almond as it is for Almond to exclude the liberal. There is a profound challenge here from both legalist and liberal to find a bond of brotherhood and a bridge of love. This is probably the most difficult and exasperating kind of reconciliation. It is delicate because neither person completely respects the morals or motives of the other.

Almond, like all men, has some personal problems and needs. His confusion and loss in the Susan Simmons episode is transparent to everyone but Almond. In spite of his arrogant self-righteousness and self-inflicted martyrdom, Almond is a lonely old man. In his loneliness, he doubtlessly wonders if he paid too high a price as a young soldier when he discarded Susan over a dance.

You know that there is more to Almond's moral crusades than he says. Like all crusaders Almond has mixed-up motives. Like all self-righteous people, Almond is secretly aware of, and frightened by, his own temptations and weaknesses. Much of his rhetoric is to convince himself of his own purity by his own standards. He believes that saying it enough will make it so.

The church must be big enough for Almond, and the church must minister to him in a loving, patient way. For the church will lose something if the church drives Almond away, although he is trying to drive others away. No one will test the flexibility of the church more than an inflexible member like Almond.

10
KING HENRY THE EIGHTH

A Baptist church is an unlikely place to find King Henry, but ten to twenty times a year King Henry is there. His name is Harold Wiley. He has been to the marriage altar eight times and several of his wives have been members of the church. There are two or three Mrs. Wileys on the church roll right now.

Harold's reputation with the ladies is well known in the city. He had been married three times when he started attending church. At that time he was between wives. His last divorce had shaken him, and he came to the church looking for help. He soon joined the church, was baptized, and became an enthusiastic and involved church member.

He is an extremely handsome man. Open countenance. Big and in good shape. Athletic. Intelligent. He has wit and is an informed conversationalist. His parents are respected citizens. He is the youngest of three brothers. The Wileys own one of the largest office buildings in town, several rental properties, and have developed at least one successful shopping center. The two older brothers have never married. They live at home with the parents, and Harold usually stays with his parents between marriages.

Mr. Wiley and the two older brothers do all of the right things. They operate their businesses without fanfare. Their employees are well paid, and they work for the Wileys until retirement. The Wileys support the proper candidates and the proper causes. They are the kind of conservative businessmen who become wealthy and influential in every small town in America. They are not eccentric. They are not rash. They are not ostentatious or flamboyant. They are proper.

The old man was delighted when Harold married, although Harold was just a sophomore in college. The girl was from a good family. The old man wanted some Wiley heirs and the older boys had not been interested in marriage. They were not interested in women. Within a year Harold presented his father with a granddaughter and eleven months later, another granddaughter. But by that time Harold had sued for divorce.

The first divorce was an embarrassment to the Wileys. They couldn't understand it, and they used every pressure to persuade Harold to call it off. He persisted, and a few days after the divorce he married a girl who worked in a bank building that the Wileys owned. Mr. Wiley promised the first wife that he would help her support the two babies until and unless she married again. He sent her regular checks for about two years, and she married again. She still brings the two girls to see their Wiley grandparents.

Harold can't get along with the women he is married to. They fight and argue. He has a bad temper with women and more than once by his own admission, and by the police records, he has beaten his wives. Usually a beating is the reason for the divorce.

This kind of violence would surprise Harold's friends. Many of them just don't believe it. He does not have attributes of violence. Quite the contrary, he laughs a lot and is reputed to be a practical joker. He has never exploded in anger at his father or brothers. He does not lose his temper with employees. He drinks moderately and has never provoked a fight at a party. In nearly every marriage, he has lost his reason and beaten his wife. He voluntarily has gone to a psychiatrist for analysis and treatment. So far the doctors haven't helped him much.

In spite of his reputation as a wife beater, King Henry

is a successful ladies' man. Women are attracted to him and every divorce seems to enhance his sex appeal. Harold is on the move and invariably is accompanied by a woman. He does not have business luncheons, he eats lunch with a woman. He takes women out to dinner, dancing, to ball games, for drives in the country, on weekend jaunts to the lakes and mountains, and he sits with women in church.

Although his morals are questionable, he is usually married. He is not a typical playboy, flitting from one liaison to another. He believes, he says, that a man and woman who love one another should be married to one another. When he begins to date a woman regularly, he usually marries her. Eight times he has married to prove that point.

Several times his distraught wives have come to me for counsel. In every case they have described Harold as being thoughtful and interesting. They say that he is essentially a good person until he erupts in anger. His anger is always directed toward the wife and normally ends in violence. Sometimes he has beaten a wife severely enough to require hospital care. He takes them to the hospital.

Never once has a wife had him prosecuted for assault. They rarely call the police. They are not really angry with him, and they are not really afraid of him. But they dissolve the marriage because they don't want to be beaten and perhaps disfigured or crippled.

Usually a wife leaves King Henry three or four times before she divorces him. When they leave, he persistently woos them back to his bed. He is apologetic and humble. He begs forgiveness. He makes promises and assurances. One wife said that he was charming and irresistible. Another described him as a "lost little boy" after she left him.

Harold has no contact with a woman after the divorce. He will not talk on the phone. He will not go to the divorce trial. He leaves all of the settlements, alimony, and other details with his lawyer. He never talks about or complains about the settlement. He has only been the father of two children, both in his first marriage, so there are no custody or child support arrangements to be made.

Some of the ex-wives are still infatuated with Harold and will try to arrange meetings, but he refuses. Some of them have remarried but are still intrigued with Harold. One of them told me she would go back to him any time, although she is married again and has children.

Harold will not date or even talk to his ex-wives, because he thinks it would be immoral and sacrilegious.

And this brings us to King Henry and the church.

Harold Wiley is a church member. He contributes money to the church in generous amounts. He attends worship. In private conversation, he not only quotes the Bible with some accuracy but has some knowledge of theology. Harold has better perception about certain theological ideas than most laymen. He reads, asks questions, and enjoys theological discussion.

He is an informed church member. He calls the pastor on the phone to suggest certain changes in church programs. He is observant about the ushers' decorum, appreciative of a choir selection, concerned when the Scouts need canoes, analytical about the church budget, and always willing to help the poor with his time and money. Harold believes in the church. He is interested in the church.

Not that he is unaware of his dubious reputation. His marital problems do affect his influence in the church. His reputation is suspect. In spite of his obvious interest in the church, in spite of his friendly disposition with other church members, in spite of some natural talent that could be used advantageously in church programs, Harold is limited in his leadership.

The church people do not put him down. I don't know of one time that he has been insulted or one time that anyone has criticized him to his face. Of course people do talk about his marriage exploits. They do look with suspicion and unbelief at his succession of marriages.

Most church people believe in one God and one marriage. They equate the holiness of God and the sanctity of marriage. They are aware of the biblical illustrations that compare sin and disobedience to adultery and immorality. A man who is loyal to God is loyal to his wife. A man takes religious vows when he takes marriage vows. I expect that most Americans think that the entire wedding ceremony is lifted from the Bible, if not the entire ceremony, at least the "till death do us part" line.

In addition to the sanctity of marriage, church people traditionally equate divorce with sin. Protestants and Catholics have been rigid about divorce. Although the Catholics have a doctrinal position about divorce that is clearly defined, Protestants have been equally inflexible in a less-defined position.

Remarriage is another dimension. There is a segment of the church that might accept divorce but cannot accept remarriage. Divorce is unavoidable at times, these people say, but remarriage can be avoided. A person can be divorced even if they don't want the divorce. But no one can be forced to marry. Remarriage is a conscious decision. People who marry again commit adultery, and they could avoid this sin. Consequently, this group in the church makes a distinction between the divorced and the married divorcee.

Harold's church has people who fall into all categories. Some believe that he has sinned. They think he should repent. But how can a man who has been married so many times ever repent or make restitution? His attitude about divorce and marriage is obviously different from theirs. It is different from anyone that they know.

There are a few who can never overlook Harold's marriage behavior. There is no way that they can see him except as King Henry with the multiple wives. His image is fixed. He is a sinner.

Others see Harold as an attractive, fascinating man. Part of this fascination is his radical departure from the traditions about marriage. They just can't believe that this guy has actually been legally married eight times. They don't know anyone who has been married three times, much less eight. They are drawn to Harold like he was something in a sideshow. He doesn't know people feel that way, because he doesn't feel that way himself. I really don't think he believes that he is abnormal.

Most of the people are not basically concerned with his conquests and failures with women. They are aware of his marriages, but not deeply interested. When he brings a new woman to church, they notice it, they talk about it. The talk is casual.

They like him as a person. They are perplexed by his marriage behavior, but they don't pry into it or try to change it. When he attends church, there are always people to talk to. Apparently he feels comfortable.

The church is big enough for King Henry the Eighth.

Although the church can and should accommodate Harold Wiley, exclusion or excommunication would not accomplish anything—there is the dimension of ministry. It is important that the church not deal harshly with Harold. It is important that he be accepted for worship and in the membership. It is important that church people not cast the first stone. He must have some acceptance before there can be any ministry.

Harold's eight marriages are an absurd illustration of a persistent problem to the church. If few people are married eight times, thousands are divorced and remarried once or twice. These thousands confront the church every day.

The modern church must develop a family life ministry to prepare young people for marriage. The roots of Harold's inability to build a marriage probably go back into his youth. No one taught Harold how to build a home. There can be no single area of Christian education more important than teaching children how to prepare for home building.

This should be a part of our youth programs in every church.

Harold Wiley has some severe personal problems. The church should have a staff member who is trained in pastoral care who can counsel Harold effectively. If the church is not able to provide that kind of staff minister, the pastor should know where and how to refer Harold for professional help. Harold is more than a playboy, he is more than a failure with women, he is a human for whom Christ died and his life has worth. He is more than an amusing Don Juan. He deserves more from the church than our censure.

A person like Harold forces us to face the question of divorce and remarriage. Although the church can and should advocate monogamy, we cannot ignore the thousands of people in every community who are divorced and/or remarried. Perhaps no other question in this decade needs more serious discussion than the attitude of the church toward divorce.

Until we plan a ministry that will help prepare people for family living, a ministry that will help preserve the family, and until we have decided how we can minister to divorced people, we must accept Harold and his kind with love and understanding. While we are accepting him, we must give high priority to helping him.

11
THE EMPTY COMMUNION CUPS

We were trying to make the communion service more impressive. We were going to have a candlelight service. No conversation. No congregational singing. No formal prayers. No sermon.

The people were to come into the candlelit auditorium. The organ was playing soft and appropriate music. At a given time the pastor would walk behind the communion table and read the Bible story about Jesus and the twelve in the upper room at the last supper.

After a few minutes of meditation, the deacons would come to get the silver trays of bread and serve the audience. Scripture passages about the cross would be read, and then the deacons would pass again through the congregation to serve the wine (grape juice).

The deacons started toward the congregation with their trays of communion cups. I noticed on the snow white linen that covered the trays, a big blotch of purple stain and assumed that the ladies had spilled the grape juice when they filled the cups that afternoon.

After serving the congregation, the deacons returned their trays to me. I took one tray and I served each of the deacons. I sat down and the deacon chairman served me. Then I soberly raised the cup and led the congregation by saying: "As oft as you drink this cup, You do show forth the Lord's death until he comes again. Jesus said, This do, in remembrance of me." We drank the cup.

There was a strange swooshing sound.

There was no juice in the cups. They were all empty. Everyone knew his own cup was empty but assumed it was an oversight. No one wanted to break the mood or appear "out of communion," so everyone lifted their cup. But there was nothing to drink. There was some color in the bottom of each communion glass, all of the juice wasn't gone, but there were just enough drops to color the glass. Nothing to drink.

After the service, there was a lot of curiosity. What in the world could have happened? Mrs. Polk and Mrs. Floyd were embarrassed and ready to weep. They were the committee to prepare communion, and they had done their duty. When they left the building at 4:30 P.M., only three hours earlier, the cups were filled. Mrs. Polk said that the glasses filled with wine had "just looked beautiful sitting there on the table." Mrs. Polk always was proud of her work.

The mystery was solved about two hours later when Mrs. Hill called me.

"Did you all have communion at church tonight?"

"Yes we did, Mrs. Hill."

"Any problems?"

"Well, Mrs. Hill, I guess it was a problem. When we served the wine, grape juice that is, all of the cups were empty. It was strange drinking juice out of an empty cup."

"Pastor, Harvey Harold got sick about two hours ago. He's been vomiting for all that time. He's mighty sick. He's sick on grape juice. I reckon that little rascal sneaked in the church and drank all of that grape juice. I'm powerful sorry, Preacher, and I'll get Mr. Hill right over there to pay for the wine, grape juice that is."

"No, no, Mrs. Hill. Please don't try to pay for the grape juice. It doesn't cost that much and paying for it isn't the point."

"Oh, I know the point all right. I'm going to keep that little rascal out of church for one solid month, that's what

I'm going to do. He won't get near that church, you can count on that."

"Please don't punish the child, Mrs. Hill, by keeping him out of church."

Every church has a child, often a dozen or more, like Harvey Harold Hill. They are in trouble before they start to school. They keep things in an uproar. They are undisciplined, they disturb other children, they frustrate Sunday School teachers, they make noise, they take things, they come into a church like tiny tornadoes.

Sunday School teachers cannot cope with Harvey Harold. The Sunday School is not equipped for this kind of child. The teachers are all volunteers. Many of them are chosen for their piety rather than any personal teaching skills. They are not trained to motivate or discipline Harvey Harold. The Sunday School does not have the chain of command or the force of law that the public school has; the Sunday School cannot force a child to behave. All we can do is send him home.

But Sunday Schools rarely send the Harvey Harolds home. Rather, year after year patient teachers try to love him, teach him, and make him into a "good boy." A surprising number of incorrigibles stay in Sunday School, at least until their middle teens.

Harvey Harold is not from a broken home. His parents are not alcoholics. They are not on the poverty rolls. They do fuss and fight, and Mrs. Hill has called the police on Mr. Hill at least fifty times. When they fight, they both throw things, cuss, and scream, but never hit one another. They both drink but not to excess. They both work. Mrs. Hill is a cook in a downtown restaurant, and Mr. Hill drives a truck for a paving contractor. Harvey Harold is the youngest of six children. Mrs. Hill said she would like to have had a dozen, but she had to have an operation and that stopped her at six.

Mr. and Mrs. Hill brag about their children, but they

do not pay any attention to them. Harvey Harold is a neglected boy, although he has enough to eat, his house is warm, and he always has clothes to wear. Some neglected kids of Harvey Harold's age are hungry, do live in tenements, and do not have adequate clothing.

Harvey Harold kept everything in an uproar during his sojourn in Sunday School and church because he wanted attention. He did everything he could to get our notice and to attract our attention. And when kind teachers did show attention and interest in Harvey Harold, he rejected them. The attention Harvey Harold wanted and needed could only come from his parents, and they didn't give it to him.

Perhaps Mr. and Mrs. Hill were too ignorant to understand what the boy wanted. They were not sensitive to each other or to any of the children. They were not prepared or willing to give the child the interest and love that he wanted. Once or twice I tried to talk to them. I was blunt. They were not even defensive. They simply didn't understand. They worked hard to feed and clothe the boy. They sent him to school and to Sunday School. He had never been hungry. He always brought a nickel to Sunday School.

Harvey Harold dropped out of church in his early teens. I didn't see him or hear anything from him for four or five years. His parents dropped out of my range of concern, too. There were no more Hill children in our Sunday School. People still remembered the empty communion cups, and occasionally someone would ask what had happened to the boy that drank all of the communion wine, grape juice that is.

His life-style hadn't changed. He was in trouble often in junior high school. Truancy. Disrupting class. Failing grades. He was in juvenile court two or three times for minor infractions of the law. He finally quit school and got a job in a filling station. He bought a car.

Harvey Harold started dating a girl in the church and again he appeared in church. He had grown. He was not yet a man, but more man than boy. Mrs. Polk still remembered him with distaste. Most of the other people had forgotten the communion cups and the other disturbances he had caused in the Sunday School.

He came by my office one day to talk. Said that he wanted to go to vocational school and learn to be an auto mechanic. He was just eighteen but he was in love with the girl, Brenda. He thought that if he learned a trade at vocational school and got a good job he and Brenda could marry. I encouraged him in his ambitions. After he left I thought that the time we had spent with Harvey Harold had paid off. I would like to tell some of those Sunday School teachers that their patience was rewarded.

But Brenda got a new boyfriend.

I guess Harvey Harold really loved her. At least he thought that he loved her. He reverted back to his old pattern. He drove too fast and drank too much. His reputation deteriorated again. Finally he was arrested with two other teenage boys for armed robbery.

Mrs. Hill asked me to go see Harvey Harold in jail. She just couldn't believe that he had done anything like that.

I saw Brenda at church. I asked her if she had seen Harvey Harold or written him a note since he had been in jail. She said that she had not and did not intend to get mixed up with him. He was nothing but trouble. She knew that he was going to get into trouble and that was why she had broken up with him.

"He was always trying too hard. Always trying to make people notice him. He was jealous. At times, I thought he was crazy. Everywhere we went, he would do something to make people look at us. It was embarrassing. I couldn't take it," Brenda concluded.

When I visited Harvey in jail he was glad to see me.

Harvey Harold raises some questions for churchmen. Where do we miss out with families like the Hills and specifically with people like Harvey Harold? In most churches there are people like this somewhere on the edge of the church. On the edge, but never inside church life.

We persistently fail to realize that most people crave personal attention. This craving becomes an obsession to some people. As society becomes more numbered and computerized, this need for personal attention grows. Children are lost in the masses at school. They are moved from room to room, teacher to teacher, and are only a digit in a school quota system. They lose their indentity at school.

The parents both work and family life becomes frantic and hurried. Television blares and automobiles run endlessly. There is little time at home for conversation or personal attention. Mothers and Dads are busy. Nearly one third of the families do not have both parents at home. An ever increasing number of people fail to find personal attention in their family. They expect to find someone at home who is profoundly interested in them. When they realize that the family does not meet this need, they turn to the church.

This turning to the church is logical. The church has a reputation for personal interest. The church has traditionally advocated a personal experience with God. Even public and corporate worship stresses the individual and God. Pastoral care is normally one on one. Various church activities and organizations are built around small group concepts. The church has the motivation and the mission to meet this kind of human need. The church can give personal attention to people like Harvey Harold. We can give them a sense of personal worth and personal dignity. We can become family for this kind of person.

This is not a new role for the church. Historically the church has focused on persons. Urbanization and the population increase have made personal ministry more difficult, but it is not impossible. Cities are larger, churches are larger, and life is more hurried. These facts do not change the essential need of individuals for attention nor do they change the peculiar ability of the church to provide that attention.

12
"WHY ALBERT?"

Al Reynolds was a good salesman. He changed jobs too often, but he always earned money and promotions. Al isn't timid. He is well dressed, drives new cars, lives in an expensive house.

His wife Carolyn is a college graduate. She was working for an advertising agency when she married Al. She was happy and reasonably successful in her work. Carolyn is an attractive, intelligent woman. She and Al had been married eight years before their first son, Albert, was born. Fifteen months later their second son, David, was born.

David wasn't a year old when Al and Carolyn began to realize that Albert wasn't a normal child. An older physician who doubtlessly meant well kept assuring them that Albert would be all right, that he was just slow in his development. Finally they took the little boy to specialists at the university. He had brain damage—physical disability and mental retardation. There was little hope for improvement.

Little Albert did not "look" retarded. Like most parents of retarded children, Al and Carolyn rejected the doctor's diagnosis. They went home determined that Albert would in fact grow up as a normal child.

As the years passed, they could not ignore Albert's limitations and handicaps. He was severely retarded. He could not learn or retain. He was restless and hyperactive. He was a constant, twenty-four hours a day care for them. He was loud and hard to control. It was impossible to discipline him. Albert's presence and behavior dominated their lives. Everything in their family was affected by Albert.

Al and Carolyn never went out together. It was hard to get a babysitter for Albert, and when they did get a sitter, they were uneasy and anxious to get home. Eventually they gave up all social engagements and rarely visited friends and never invited people to their home.

When he was little, they would take Albert to a restaurant or even to a movie. But people stared at them. At least they thought people stared. Albert was too excited when he went out, and he called attention to himself by his behavior. It was easier for them to stay at home.

Their circle of friends decreased. Al had friends that he met at work. Carolyn occasionally phoned old friends, but she never went to see any of them. She never invited them to her home.

Al attended some basketball games. He was in a civic club that had luncheon meetings. Every Thursday night he stayed with the boys and Carolyn drove twenty miles to visit her aging mother. Her mother visited them once a year on Thanksgiving Day. Saturday mornings Carolyn went to the shopping center. She bought groceries and clothes for the boys. Occasionally she would buy clothes for herself, but she didn't really need any except to go shopping in.

Carolyn and Al learned to hate one another. Often parents of retarded children try to place blame. They may blame God. They may blame the attending physician. Usually they blame themselves. Carolyn was bitter and angry with Al. She was convinced that he was immoral, that he had been unfaithful to her during the early years of their marriage and that God had punished Al's adultery by sending the retarded child.

Al did not admit adultery to Carolyn, but it was a fact. The more she accused him, the more he denied it. His denial and lying compounded his guilt. Carolyn nagged him constantly. He dreaded going home from work, but he felt guilty when he wasn't with the boys. So he sat at home every night in front of a television set.

Carolyn and Al were miserable, friendless, and extremely lonely. They did not, apparently could not, cope with Albert. They made no attempt to get him in a school for the retarded. They were obsessed with caring for him but did nothing to help him. At the same time, they knew that their marriage had disintegrated. They did not sleep together. They did not talk. They lived in hostility.

The public school saved David. Neither parent knew how to play with David. They didn't know how to talk to David. They didn't know how to accept David. He was a normal child, and their attention was completely focused on Albert. Their emotions were controlled by their growing hostility to one another. David was a neglected child.

Fortunately his sixth-grade teacher was a sensitive, intelligent, Christian man. He was kind and interested. The boy responded and confided in the teacher. They became friends. The teacher invited David to his home, took him to ball games, and brought him into our Sunday School. Eventually the teacher got to know Al and Carolyn well enough to get into their home. A few visits in the home convinced the teacher that this family was in desperate trouble and the church could help.

There are numerous ways that churches can help families that are in trouble. Churches have traditionally ministered in times of death. A generation ago church friends "kept the wake," went to funerals, served as pallbearers, and carried food to the bereaved. Churches have helped during times of illness, fire, or flood, and have always been concerned for widows and orphans.

If Albert had been dead instead of retarded, the church would have known what to do. If Carolyn had been in the hospital, the church could have taken Al and the boys food and the members could have stayed at the hospital with Carolyn.

But what can the church do for a retarded child, a broken marriage, an angry mother, a neglected boy, a hostile father? Is there any way that the church can move into this family with love and actually minister to their needs? The school teacher believed that the church could. In fact, he believed that the church had the answers, the people, and the motivation for this ministry of reconciliation.

We started with David, the normal, but neglected boy. Through the Sunday School, we brought him into a Scout Troop. The Sunday School and Scouts gave him exposure to Christian men. Men who were not bitter and hostile like his father. He learned about God. He went on hikes and camping trips. He learned about the outdoors and about getting along with people. He learned Bible verses, hymns, and prayers. He learned to swim and to tie knots.

Al reluctantly attended the first scouting awards banquet. He enjoyed the banquet, and David was proud of his father. In fact, David had never been as proud!

A few weeks later David made a profession of faith and wanted to be baptized. Al and Carolyn said he could be baptized if that was what he wanted. The schoolteacher's wife insisted that she stay with Albert so that Al and Carolyn could attend the baptism. They protested, made excuses, and finally refused. But when the teacher's wife came to the house, they went to the baptism. The first time in eight years that they had gone to church together.

For years we have had a special Sunday School class for retarded children. Our next goal was to get Albert into that class. The teachers in that class must have visited Al and Carolyn a dozen times. They phoned. They wrote Albert attractive invitations. Finally Al and Carolyn decided to let Albert come to Sunday School once. Al brought him, sat outside the door, and took him home after Sunday School. Albert enjoyed the class immensely. But they wouldn't bring him back for three months. The patient concern of Albert's teachers influenced the parents, and Albert returned to the special class.

The class made dramatic changes in Albert. This boy had been hidden all of his life. He was never around other children. He was never with adults. No one had ever tried to teach him. He had never been taught music in a group; he had never been in a group. Although he could not retain facts and although he is very hard to discipline, he does have some capacity to remember people and a great capacity for joy.

Al and Carolyn both recognized and acknowledged the changes in their boys. They were courteous to our church people and were appreciative of our ministry. They always expressed gratitude, and Al would mail the pastor a monthly check for the church budget. He said that was the least he could do.

We were delighted that we could help the boys. The hostility and alienation between Al and Carolyn still existed. Although they both were better able to accept the boys, they had made no progress in accepting one another. There was no evidence that they had or intended to establish any relationship with God.

It was a crisis, as it often is, that gave us an opportunity to minister to Al and Carolyn personally. Al lost his job. Although he had been a leading salesman for his company for more than a dozen years, a change of ownership caused him to get fired. He was out of work. With their other problems, Al and Carolyn had never before faced financial insecurity. He was nearly fifty. It was hard to find a job. After six or eight weeks, he was about to panic.

He came by to talk to me. He wanted to know if he could use my name as a reference. I told him that I would be glad to help, but I actually didn't know much about him. He opened up and talked for more than two hours. He told me about the boys, about his guilt, about his alienation from Carolyn, and about their hostility. He talked about his goals and frustrations, saying that he had never told anyone before.

Some men in the church helped, and we were able to find Al a job. Church members can do this. The pastor was able to help Al and Carolyn understand that God doesn't arbitrarily pick out little babies like Albert and handicap them to punish adultery. God doesn't do mean things to people. A lot of counseling, witnessing, and loving led Al and Carolyn to the Lord and to forgiveness. Al has been a deacon in our church for a couple of years, and Carolyn sings in the choir.

Albert is still retarded. David is working in a local insurance office. Al and Carolyn still argue. They still get mad at one another. At times they revert back to blaming. Albert is hard for them to cope with. They wasted more than a dozen years in anger and frustration. But a sensitive schoolteacher and a caring church did make a difference.

13
TONY THE MOTHER

Tony made an appointment to see me. She is a high school senior. Her parents are active members of our church. Her dad is a successful real estate developer, her mother is a shy housewife. Tony is not particularly attractive. Her high school career has been relatively bland. I thought that she wanted to talk to me about school or perhaps her role in the church.

I was wrong. Tony was pregnant. She wanted to talk about the alternatives that she had as an unwed teenage pregnant girl.

In spite of a more tolerant society and increased knowledge about birth control, the Tonys multiply at an alarming rate. More sex education and more sophisticated young people have not eliminated the fact of pregnant teenage girls. Often these girls seek help from a clergyman as they try to work their way through the dilemma of an unexpected and unwanted pregnancy.

Tony was considering an abortion. The Supreme Court decision in 1973 had changed the Kentucky abortion law. Tony knew some local girls who had gone to New York for an abortion before the state law was changed. They weren't gone very long. In a few days they were back home, and everything seemed all right. It seemed like an abortion was easily arranged here in Tony's hometown, or she could go to another city. It wasn't very complicated.

Tony said this would be the easiest way out.

She did have some hesitation. It would cost money. She would have to pay the doctor who did the abortion, plus fees and hospital bills. She would have to tell her parents. They might not put up the money. Like most pregnant teenagers, she didn't want her parents to know she was pregnant. But there wasn't any other way to get the money.

Tony told me that one friend of hers, Patsy, had an abortion. Patsy was pretty sick about a week after she came home. She was in the hospital five or six days. She had a lot of pain. Patsy said it was an infection. Patsy cried a lot. Tony thought maybe Patsy was just emotionally upset, but it might have been an infection. Tony was afraid that an abortion was more dangerous than some people said. She was afraid that she might get an infection and die. This was a genuine fear.

Tony was sure that she would be emotionally upset. She thought that an unborn baby was in fact a human. Although she didn't plan to get pregnant, she believed that the new baby in her womb was a person. She felt like an abortion was an act of destruction. The destruction of a human. This thought repelled her. She became tense as she discussed it. If the unborn baby wasn't a human, what was it? Tony said that she wasn't as religious as I might think, but she didn't like the idea of taking a life.

Because an abortion was distasteful, she had thought about marriage. The father of the baby was another teenager. His name was Dan. She said that I didn't know Dan. She didn't know him very well herself.

Dan would finish high school this year. He wasn't a good student. He was working part-time as a bus boy at Howard Johnson's. He didn't have any future plans. He did not want to get married, but he said that he would marry to give the baby a name.

Tony wasn't sure that a name was that important. Why give the baby a name of a boy who doesn't want the baby? Is it important to give a baby just any name, or should it be the name of a man who loves and wants the child?

Marriage should be more than this. Tony has a higher ideal about marriage. She thinks that marriages should be planned. A couple should love one another. There should be a commitment and some compatibility. Dan and Tony do not have a commitment to one another.

Tony has some fears about marriage. She isn't ready to leave her parents. She isn't prepared for marriage. She wants to get married when the right man comes along at the right time. Dan isn't the right man, and this isn't the right time. Tony says that the marriage will fail.

Marriage is the easiest way out. It is the most obvious solution. The young couple does give the baby a name. They give the baby a home, a set of married parents.

Unfortunately most of these marriages do not last. The baby is born into a fragile marriage. When the marriage breaks up, the baby grows up in a broken home. The baby has a name but does not have a home during the important growing years. If the mother divorces and marries again, the baby will probably take the new father's name.

Tony thinks an unwanted marriage is as unfortunate as an unwanted baby. She doesn't want to marry. She doesn't want to marry Dan. Dan doesn't want to marry her. They both have agreed that marriage is an alternative and is the most acceptable option. Society will approve of their marriage and the wedding license will legalize their unhappiness. The baby will have a name. Of course, some of these marriages do work out. Some of these couples do grow and mature together. Some of these marriages do last.

When a marriage begins under these circumstances, there may be an added incentive to make it last. Occasionally a couple will be more determined to work out problems. This determination will provide motivation and patience for an enduring marriage.

Tony has considered having the baby at home and rearing the child with her own name and without a husband. She says that some famous women have done that, and she thinks it could be done.

She would have to get some help from her parents. They don't know that she is pregnant, and they will blow their minds when they find out. But they do love her. They have always been good to her. They will be angry, frustrated, and hurt, but they won't turn her out. At least, she doesn't think they will turn her out.

Her dad could afford to pay the bills. Her mother could help her when the baby is small. They might even be glad to have a baby around the house after the initial shock and embarrassment has worn off. Her mother is young enough to take care of the baby, and Tony could get a job. Then when "Mr. Right" comes along, she will get married, and "Mr. Right" would be a father to the child. If "Mr. Right" loves her, he will accept the child.

There are thousands who raise children without a husband. They are divorced or widows. They don't seem to have as many problems as they had in an unhappy marriage. Tony thinks that she could take care of the baby and give it all that she has, providing that her parents will help.

If her parents will not agree to this arrangement, her options are narrow. She would have to get a place to live. Perhaps she could draw some welfare money. Everyone accuses the government of paying for illegitimate children. She could get some of that welfare money. Eventually she could get a job or get married. The baby would at least be loved, and Tony would not be encumbered with an unhappy husband or complaining, embarrassed parents.

The baby would grow up under a stigma though. It wouldn't be long before he knew that he was illegitimate. This would affect him. If her parents raise him, it will not be normal. If he is raised as a welfare baby, it will not be normal. Tony thinks that this alternative would be extremely unfair to the baby. Although it is a possibility, she rejects it because it will hurt the baby.

She knows that she could go to a home for unwed mothers, have the baby, and allow someone to adopt it. Tony has a good friend who is an adopted child. Her friend is a happy, well-adjusted young man. He was adopted when he was eight weeks old. His parents are devoted to him. Tony thinks that they are nice people.

If she goes this route, she will still have to tell her parents she is pregnant. This is her immediate fear. But this is inescapable. With any alternative, she must tell her parents. And she must accept the embarrassment and the pain of telling. Others will find out about her pregnancy. The sooner her parents know, the sooner they will accept her.

She does not want to leave home to go to a home for unwed mothers. She thinks she will be lonely, and she will. She has never been away from home for any length of time. They may send her to another city.

Tony doesn't like the idea of "giving the baby away." The baby is a part of her. It will have some of her features. It will inherit certain traits from Tony. When it is born, it will already be something of her. She will never watch the baby grow. If she allows someone to adopt the baby, they will see its first tooth, they will watch the baby take the first step, and some other woman will be that baby's mother forever.

Giving up the baby is a traumatic idea for this teenager. She feels, or thinks she feels, a mysterious identity with this unborn child.

Tony has faced her alternatives. There is no easy answer to her problem. There is no decision that is painless and pleasant. She is in a bind. She will always wonder why or how this happened to her. She will wonder if she made the right decision. The right decision for the baby. And for Tony.

A few days later she called me.

Her parents had insisted that she marry Dan. Dan's parents agreed. They wanted me to marry them. She and Dan had "decided" that they loved one another and that they could build a happy home. The parents thought this was best. They would tell people that they married six months ago. The baby would have a name.

Tony, the pregnant, unwed teenager, is one of the most perplexing persons that the church will try to minister to. The plight of the pregnant teenager reminds the church that there must be an enlarged and more effective sex education program in the church. We have tried to teach our children about sex with severe self-imposed limitations. We have couched our teaching in language that they cannot understand. We have been apologetic and embarrassed, and they know we are unsure.

Our young people are living in a sex-saturated society. They get sex education in school; they are deluged with pornography and perversion; they are overwhelmed with sex. But they are still children who need to be told the truth about sex with all of the moral, emotional, as well as biological ramifications of sexual behavior. This kind of education is a valid part of the Christian ministry.

Education will not eliminate all of the unwed mothers from our society or from our church family. As long as passion can exceed self-control in humans, we will have pregnant teenage girls and unwanted babies.

The church must be big enough to accept the unwed mother. She desperately needs love, not condemnation. She needs Christians who will stick with her through the miserable time of decision and the months of pregnancy. Every alternative she faces has definite moral and religious implications. It is grossly unfair to leave her alone to struggle through these profound moral decisions without the strong friendship and love of her church.

Although the decision is ultimately up to Tony, the church can help her see the alternatives, and regardless of her decision, the church can continue to love and accept her.

14

A NEW SONG

When I became a pastor, an experienced churchman told me that the music department in the church was the "war department." Most churches have volunteer choirs. Actually most volunteer choirs aren't too bad, musically. These volunteers are willing to rehearse and rehearse and this music is usually satisfactory.

There is always room for battle though. Choirs like attention and recognition. They are usually late to the worship service because every choir director tries to polish the selection just before service time. He rarely can select his singers, or audition them, and so he invariably has some who just can't sing. These monotones always sound worse to him in that preservice warm-up. There is something about music that makes performers sensitive. That is the reason for battle, sensitivity.

The first time I met Maude Rinehart she was teaching a ladies Bible class. Old Mrs. Johnson, the regular teacher of that class, had told me that she was inviting this young neighbor to be guest teacher. Mrs. Johnson wanted me to come by and speak to her neighbor. She said that her neighbor was unhappy in her church and was looking for a new church home. So I peeked into the room of the Fidelis Class.

Too late. Maude Rinehart was already teaching. She wasn't a young woman, but I remembered that Mrs. Johnson was past seventy-five and anyone younger than sixty looked young to her. Not that Maude Rinehart was old; she was about fifty. It would have been embarrassing to leave, so I just sat down to listen.

Maude Rinehart was quite a speaker! She was teaching the Fidelis Class with genuine skill. She was prepared. She had a good vocabulary, some wit, and a winning smile. She illustrated her points effectively. Her voice was loud enough for the old ladies to hear, but it wasn't unpleasant. I decided that morning that she was one of the finest teachers that I had ever heard.

After class, Mrs. Johnson introduced me to Maude Rinehart. I complimented her teaching and went on to the worship service. That morning Maude and her husband P. J. joined the church. It appeared to be a good addition to the church.

If volunteer choir singers are a problem, volunteer Sunday School teachers are a disaster. Often Sunday School enrollment in a church is larger than church membership. We can get people into our Sunday School, but the secret of an effective school is the teacher. We cannot find many skilled volunteer teachers. Most of our churches elect teachers who are willing to teach. We do not ask for anything in a teacher but willingness.

Maude Rinehart was skilled. A skilled Sunday School teacher. How about that?

Some teachers don't know the difference between King Saul and Saul of Tarsus. They talk about Noah and his arch. Jesus was without sin because he did not marry. One teacher thought that B.C. meant Before Communism and A.D. meant After Democracy. Sunday School teachers are too often poorly prepared, superstitious, careless, dogmatic, and are most often boring beyond description.

Maude Rinehart was different.

But Maude wouldn't teach. She told me that she wouldn't teach because she was a singer. Not a choir singer. Not a duet or trio singer. She was a soloist. She said that she couldn't mix teaching and singing. Teaching would hurt her voice.

Nothing could hurt Maude's singing voice! After hearing her sing the first time, I realized that she was probably the worst singer that I had ever heard. People in the church thought that she was the worst singer in the city. One of the men decided that she was the poorest singer in America, if not in the entire history of the church. Words cannot adequately describe Maude's songs. Sharp. Flat. Discordant. Shrill. Scrape. The sounds were unbelievable.

It was more than a bad sound. Maude's entire appearance changed when she sang. Someone had told her to roll her eyes, and she rolled her eyes like a Kewpie doll. Her eyes were blank. She didn't see anything, but she rolled her eyes. She puckered her mouth. No one could pucker to sing like Maude. This affected her diction, and she looked like she was waiting in the kissing booth at the county fair. With all of these facial contortions, Maude also tried to smile when she sang. It's hard to smile and pucker at the same time, but Maude tried. The smile was a puckered leer, but everyone knew that Maude was trying to smile.

Maude was not only a poor singer, she not only looked ridiculous, she made rotten selections. Her taste in music was strange. She occasionally "offered" an old familiar hymn. Sometimes she would sing a song with a gospel beat, but Maude had no rhythm and a country song would sound like an anthem. She could take a devotional song and give it a modern beat. Maude said that she liked to innovate. People do not like for singers to change songs they know. They like familiar songs. They do not want singers innovating, experimenting with, and changing the old songs.

It was offensive. Maude's entire performance was offensive.

Apparently Maude was unaware of this. She acted like she was a gifted singer. She told people that everyone should use their God-given talents, and she had promised the Lord years ago that she would always sing for the Lord when anyone asked her to. When no one asked, Maude was not one to hide her candle under a bushel—she asked to be asked. At least twice a month she would remind the music director that it had been awhile since she had sung.

She worked on her music. She practiced in front of a mirror. She bought new clothes to sing in and always had her hair styled before she sang in church. Once she called me at midnight to tell me that the Lord had given her words to sing. She wrote words about the crucifixion of Jesus to sing to the tune of "Beautiful Dreamer." She wrote a baptismal song to the tune of "Flow Gently Sweet Afton." At Christmas she sang and narrated a story about the Wise Men to the tune of "Old Black Joe."

It was terrible! Months of Maude's music turned into years. It was embarrassing when there were visitors at church. The children in the congregation would giggle and poke one another. I would sit on the pulpit in misery and apprehension. The choir was angry and hostile. The music directors were frustrated.

No one could insult Maude. Perhaps no one tried. The music director and I tried to put her off. We scheduled music weeks in advance to discourage her. But it was hard to stop her. She was determined to sing. Until she had to get false teeth. Her new dentures were not designed for puckering and singing. Maude never sang another solo. The dentist was a member of the church and people privately accused him of building the new teeth so that Maude couldn't sing again. He never denied it. Maude's singing career ended.

Maude took the Fidelis Class when Mrs. Johnson broke her hip. She was a fine Sunday School teacher. Probably the best teacher in the entire church. She should have been teaching instead of singing, and everyone knew that but Maude.

After three or four years of musical retirement, Maude developed a terminal cancer. The diagnosis was grim. I went by the hospital after surgery, and Maude was half awake.

P. J., her husband, was down getting coffee. Maude and I talked.

She had expected bad news and wasn't surprised when the doctor told her. She talked to me about P. J. and the daughters. Both daughters were married, and Maude was expecting to become a grandmother. Maude told me that she wanted to live long enough to see that first grandchild. She knew there would be other grandchildren, and P. J. would be a mighty proud grandfather, but she wanted to live long enough to see at least one grandchild.

Maude said that she didn't believe in making bargains with the Lord or asking for unnecessary things, but she was going to pray enough, long enough and hard enough, to see that grandchild.

They kept her in the hospital. Church people visited her. She got a lot of flowers, cards, and candy. She was always cheerful and pleasant when she had visitors. People said her morale was great. The nurses liked her and the doctors were proud of her. More than once P. J. and I had a long talk in the waiting room at the hospital. P. J. loved and admired Maude. He knew that she was fighting to live long enough to see that grandchild.

Cancer is relentless. Often the pain is agonizing. The side effects of the disease and the treatment are ugly and miserable. There is an atmosphere in a cancer patient's room. There is a smell. A feeling. Cancer patients develop an attitude. Their families develop an attitude. It's different with a coronary. It's different with other diseases. The cancer room is depressing. Stifling. Smothering. I've seen it too often, and I have a deep loathing and revulsion.

Maude was the exception. Her body wasted away. She was eventually too weak to feed herself. She couldn't keep her dentures in. She was losing her hair and her face was swollen. She couldn't control her bowels, and her left arm wouldn't move. Her skin was tight and had an ugly sheen. She didn't try to talk. The doctor thought she would go into a coma. But he was wrong. The disease progressed and Maude stayed conscious.

The grandchild was born.

I was there when P. J. told Maude. She tried to smile. She mumbled something to me. I bent over the bed, and Maude said: "Preacher, the Lord and I are even. I've prayed hard twice in my life. I prayed that he would make me a singer, and I prayed to see my grandchild. I got one out of two wishes. That's not bad."

Two or three days later Maude did go into a coma and then she died. I conducted her funeral. I thought once about telling them at the funeral that Maude knew all along that she couldn't sing. That although her solo attempts were ridiculous to us, her trying wasn't ridiculous to her. More than anything, Maude wanted to sing.

At the funeral I realized that the mourners weren't thinking about Maude's terrible solos. They were remembering her as a warm, friendly, faithful friend. A teacher. A woman who endured great pain without whimpering. They were remembering her as a grandmother.

Sure, they would remember her terrible music. But she tried. She tried and failed. They all could identify with that. They had tried and failed, too. They knew all about failure. Don't we all?

And what is the church about anyway if it is not about trying and failing. One of the words translated *sin* means missing the mark. The Bible says that we all have sinned, all have missed the mark, all have tried and failed.

Church work demands and deserves the best that we have. There is no excuse for shoddy service to God. We must never be content with a second-class effort. At the same time the church has inhibited and discouraged so many sincere people by an aura of professionalism. We have incorrectly and inconsistently talked about professionalism in ministry.

Of course, church music would be better if church musicians were trained and talented musicians. The Sunday School would be more professional if we had trained teachers. We can employ professional fund raisers to collect money, professional evangelists to convert the lost, and professional counselors to advise the troubled. But the essence of the church is the ministry of the laity. We owe these people the very best kind of help in developing skills in evangelism, education, music, and counseling. Constant progress is being made in training laymen. The professional church staff should be committed to this kind of enabling.

At the same time we must remember that every church has people like Maude. They may not have the skills or gifts. Their contribution may not be constructive. They may miss their calling and distort their talent. But they are children of God who deserve more than our criticism and judgement.

The ministry of the laity must be big enough to allow people to err. It must be big enough to tolerate ineptness and failure. If the church insists on professionalism in every area, we will soon relegate the lay ministry to the outer limits. There must be room in our churches for those who try and fail in the areas of service and ministry.

15
"THE CHURCH IS PEOPLE"

When I became a pastor, I was eighteen. Although my parents had taken me to the little church in my hometown all of my life, I wasn't prepared for the pastoral ministry. I was mature enough to know that my home church was composed of people. All kinds of people. At eighteen I thought that my countyseat hometown in rural Kentucky was unique. Special. Unusual.

I thought the church that called me would be different, the people would be different. Surely under my leadership the church would not be bogged down and limited by personality conflicts. We would not argue about trivial things. We would not be caught up in church politics. I honestly believed that the people would come together "with one mind in one place" and like Pentecost, the Spirit of God would do wonders in that place.

A quarter century has passed. I have been pastor of three churches during that time. My zeal for and excitement about the ministry hasn't changed. I think a pastor has a more interesting life than anyone else. There have been times, many times, when I was so discouraged and tired that I would have traded jobs with anyone in town. There have been times when people have so angered and frustrated me, that I was ready to quit. There have been times, many times, when "spiritual things" and religious rites were as empty to me as they have ever been to an agnostic.

Even in those periods of doubt and depression, I have

been fascinated by the people in the church. It has been the people with their weakness and strength, their foolishness and wisdom, their pettiness and greatness that have held me.

It has been said that the church is irrelevant and in decline. This proposition has been made so often that it has become a cliche with churchmen and the secular commentators. Like many oft-repeated phrases, a close examination may reveal error.

The church is condemned for a hesitant posture about race relations, war, poverty, and other dramatic social and moral concerns of this generation. The church has been reluctant to enter those areas of controversy. Oft . . . at the point of entry the church has been criticized, for her judgment has been questionable and the timing has been bad. Too often the social concern of the church has been expressed by the hierarchy and has had little support of the lay people.

At times the church has been pompous and patronizing in passing resolutions, making studies, preparing papers, conducting conferences, appropriating funds, and lobbying for legislation. Some of these activities have left the grass roots laity frustrated and angry.

The mass media has publicized certain churchmen: Martin Luther King; the Beregan brothers; Father Groppi; Bishop Pike; Billy Graham; Norman Vincent Peale; Billy James Hargis; and Oral Roberts. These people have all been in the news, representing every shade of thought about current events. They all have a following. They all stir the imagination, and they all attract loyal disciples who contribute money and energy to the causes espoused by the publicized churchmen.

There may be a kind of irrelevance in the publicized religionist, too. Although blacks identify closely with King and still consider him as their most articulate spokesman of the past twenty years, the average black churchman in

Memphis and Los Angeles will not concede that King represented his (the individual churchman) religious experience. The more conservative may cheer Hargis, send him money, and pray for his crusade. But the average conservative does not feel that Hargis is actually a part of his religious experience. Even Graham, who represents millions in the middle, is not closely identified with an individual's religious experience. Most religious people express their religion in their local church. They identify personally with their pastor, priest, rabbi, and with other members of their local church.

The institutional church may not change the American scene as much as people would like. It seems impossible to mobilize more than 120 million church members. No cause, no injustice, no personality can unite that massive group or motivate that group to common purpose. If the church is dying or dead because the church will not unite as a political or social reform institution, then the church died at birth. For the church has never had that kind of relevance.

Others charge the church with spiritual and personal ineptitude. This deficiency is being attacked by church renewal, the charismatic movement, and the Jesus Freaks. The proposition in this complaint is that the church has failed to use the spiritual resources available. The church has become muscle bound with organization and committees. The church does not actually change men. Men are void, empty, lost, and lonely. The traditional church approach has left them spiritually hungry.

Prayer and Bible study groups appear overnight. Renewal books become best sellers. Housewives, physicians, teachers, businessmen, and students meet weekly in homes for lengthy prayer and sensitivity sessions. They confess sin. They pray for one another. They practice a kind of religious group therapy.

Tongue-speaking, healing, and prophecy are often related to these groups. They are heavy on the Holy Spirit and the "gifts" of the Holy Spirit. This charismatic experience gives them an excitement and zeal that they have not had. They become very evangelical and enthusiastic about sharing their spiritual experience with others. They have their heroes, too. These heroes are usually writers and talented speakers who appear at rallies, retreats, and renewal conferences.

The renewal groups are usually very critical of the organized church. They condemn the church as being dead, without purpose, and irrelevant. They see no real value in the traditional church functions of worship, preaching, and teaching. They think that this has been superficial at best. They accuse main-line churchmen of deliberately denying spiritual experience and release to the people.

The church renewal people have little or no concern about social reform. They do not criticize the church for that kind of institutional immobility. They are primarily concerned with spiritual experience—a man and God. Their direction is perpendicular, they look to God. They have little horizontal interest, they are not preoccupied with, in fact they seem unaware of, their neighbor.

The charismatic, small-group people do not pretend to reach the masses. Their purpose is the small group—selected people. They make no effort to saturate. Their thesis is to take a few ordinary, empty people and fill them. This may take years. But time is not important. The individual is important.

The approach of other groups have many of the attributes of the church renewal and charismatic movements. They are outside of the traditional church. They are evangelical. Their programs are pointed toward the masses.

Where the renewal groups spend months in intense personal dialogue, other groups build their witness on street ministry. This is an almost casual "witness." They give testimony, recite some Scripture, pass a pamphlet, say a prayer, and move on to the next prospect. Some of those witnesses claim thirty converts in one day on a college campus or on a beach.

Even with the wide publicity given to such groups as the Jesus People, small groups, and the charismatic movement, they do not represent the majority of the religious people in America today. Their movements grow. Their disciples are devoted and enthusiastic. They have brought a new vitality, and corresponding controversy, to the religious scene.

But they have not and will not replace the local church.

I simply do not believe that the local church will die. I do not believe it will be discarded because it is being criticized. I do not believe it will be replaced because certain people find it inadequate, inept, or irrelevant. History is on the side of the church. The church has had more serious threats and has endured. God does not have to operate through the church, but it has pleased him to operate that way thus far.

The church has been clumsy. The church has been harsh and rigid. The church has been timid and silent. The church has been a reflection of culture and the status quo. The church has been sterile and impotent. The church has failed miserably to be what she claims to be. The church has held out false hope, has ignored human need, has sinned blatantly, has turned men away empty.

But the church has always been interesting.

This is the human explanation for twenty centuries of existence. The church has always been people. All kinds of people. The good and bad. The church has members who are seventeen and seventy. Members who teach in universities and drive trucks. Harlots and housewives. Hungarians, hillbillies, and steel workers. The church claims Albert Schweitzer, Robert E. Lee, and the local garbage collectors. Church members are tall and short, obese and skinny. The church belongs to Fran Tarkenton, George Romney, Lester Maddox, and the waitress at the coffee shop. The bus driver and the man who owns the bus company. The paper boy and the publisher.

No other institution has such an array of persons. The church collects them from every place in the city. They gather week by week for worship and ministry. Their motives for attending are mixed and poorly defined. Their religious feelings and convictions are even more varied and unclear. They are a conglomeration of hurts, joys, ambitions, failures, hostilities, convictions, and expectations.

They do not have to attend the church. They do not have to join the church. They do not have to give money to their church. They do not have to come back next Sunday. What they do is voluntarily done. There is no reprisal, no coercion, no way that they can be forced into the church.

I believe in the church. I'm intrigued by the people. Lest we forget the people, this book gives some insight into the people in a local church. And as long as there are people like these, there will be a church.

The church will touch all kinds of people and in all kinds of life situations. Many of these that the church touches, the church will hold. They will be held by the church because the church met a particular need at a particular time. Meeting that need is called ministry. And as long as the church can and will minister to human need, the church will exist in our society.

Meeting need may be done poorly by the church. The church will make mistakes and give wrong answers. The church will err because the church will try to meet the need with poorly prepared volunteers. There is a movement in the churches to train the clergy and laity in certain ministering skills. This kind of emphasis has greatly improved the quality of ministry, but there are still glaring weaknesses in the church.

There are other human needs that the church has not defined. There are people in our communities whose need is overlooked and ignored. Some of our churches do not know how to cope with specific human problems. Others know that ministry to certain people is complex, discouraging, and controversial. We pass by on the other side because it is tough to minister in a particular situation.

Certain churches in this decade structure ministry to reach specific groups of people. Other churches touch and help unusual people without a special structure or organization. The very nature of the local churches provides an opportunity for ministry that is unlike the extra-church groups and that is unlike governmental agencies. The church has the equipment and the motivation to do things for people to the glory of God. This is consistent with the purpose of the church and it is the practical reason that the church has existed without interruption for twenty centuries. Men need the church and that one fact guarantees her existence in every generation.

The church can improve her ministry. She can train her ministers better. She can become sensitive to individuals. She can become more tolerant and more devoted to a ministry of reconciliation. She can become less rigid and more inclusive. There is always a need for a larger ministry. But I have a conviction that the average local church does more for people casually than most organizations do by design. The church exists for people, not people for the church.

SUMMARY

Now you have met the people. They are in your church and your community. The church meets a special need in their life. It is "their" church.

There is something about the church that attracts them. They hold on to the church and the genuine church holds on to them. There are no church circles that circle them in or out. No walls. No fences. No barricades. No rules. No regulations. No lines, real or imaginary, that circle them in or out.

We try to understand them. We try to instruct them. We try to accept them. We admire them, are embarrassed by them, frustrated with them. They become family. They make us angry. They share our dreams. We laugh and cry with them. We enjoy their good times and weep when they weep.

By God's grace, we learn to love them.

All of the time while we are trying to accept and love them, they are trying to accept us. They could write a book about us, too. They see our weaknesses and failures, our fumbling and our absurd inconsistencies. They are aware of "us," for we are all in this "church thing" together. The church is not "them." The church is "us." The church is people. Jesus built his church on people.